THE WINDOW OF AFFORDABILITY

A PRIMER FOR BAY AREA FIRST-TIME HOME BUYERS

BY STEVEN A. LYONS

Special thanks to: Lisa Ouya and Chris Taylor of the California Association of Realtors, Claudia Kim of Cal-Bay Mortgage, Robyn Brode, Bree Johnston, Mom, Robert Skinner, and Joan Westley.

Cover Design: Sandy Biagi
Window Illustration: Doug McCarthy
Seesaw Cartoon: Carlos Alden

ISBN 0-9618084-2-X

Library of Congress Catalog Card Number: 89 - 51771

Printed in the United States of America

STRATOSPHERE PUBLISHING

7118 Westmoorland Drive
Berkeley, California 94705
(415) 486-1310

The real estate industry is constantly changing. You can help others like yourself by calling to my attention any outdated material. Also, if you have a particularly bad experience with any of the organizations listed in the reference section, let me know. Finally, send any material appropriate for the reference section to Stratosphere Publishing.

PART ONE

SHOULD I BUY?
CAN I BUY?

During the first half of the 1980s, the usual flow of first-time home buyers into the real estate market slowed to a trickle, held in check by a dam of high interest rates. However, the plummeting of interest rates later in the 80s sent a flood of first-time home buyers rushing into the housing market. Over most of the past decade many renters have assumed that the American dream of home ownership is out of their reach, and have therefore remained ignorant of the complex world of real estate. This book is a crash course on real estate, addressed to those who want to take advantage of the present window of affordability. By the end of this primer, the real estate novice will have gained insight into whether he or she should or can buy, and also begin to understand the whole morass of financing a foray into the real estate jungle.

This is a four-part book. Part One investigates two questions: Should I buy? Can I buy? Part Two discusses house hunting and purchase offers. Part Three examines creative home buying, and the book closes with a large reference and resource section.

SHOULD I BUY?

The first question the potential buyer must ask is not "Can I buy?" but rather "Should I buy?" There is no law that requires every human being to stop fooling around and settle down with a nice deed of trust by age 28, regardless of what your mother says.

Initially, ignore whether or not you can afford a home. To determine whether you should buy a house, ask yourself "What do I want? What are my goals? What will make me happy?" Make a list of your answers to these questions. Objectively scrutinize your list. Would home ownership enhance your aspirations or inhibit them?

To determine if home ownership will help you down the path to your goals and dreams, carefully consider all the ramifications of owning a home. Subsequent sections revel in the delights of home owning. But let's pause for a moment to consider home ownership's negative side. What should you be considering now to avoid disappointment in the future?

Before entering into holy matrimony with a house, consider its five troublesome children, which shall be yours to have and to hold.

Before you own a home, you must buy it first. The substantial time investment to find and purchase a home is the first troublesome child. Reading this book is just the beginning of that time investment. After splashing about in a sea of real estate books and seminars, you then must spend innumerable weekends looking at houses and talking to realtors. Upon finding a house you're interested in, you must do exhaustive research on the home, make offers, counter offers, talk to banks, and apply for loans. If you are over-committed in other areas of your life, perhaps the added burden of a housing search should be postponed.

Once you've bought the house, then its physical upkeep is your responsibility, which is another of the home's children. If you have a penchant toward funky little houses, remember they usually come equipped with funky little toilets, which are your responsibility when they explode. No more calling the landlord when the roof leaks or when the cockroaches become unbearable. To maintain its health, this 20,000 cubic-foot baby nurses on your money and your time. Do you want such a demanding child in your life right now?

Along with the physical upkeep of the house comes the financial upkeep of the mortgage, which is the third infant. If your after-tax monthly loan payment is substantially higher than your current monthly rent payment, carefully weigh the effect of that financial hardship on your future. Owning a house may be a bad idea if, for example, you plan to work only part time next year or if you hope to save money to buy a boat. As will be seen, by deducting mortgage interest from your taxes, the monthly loan payment may approximate your current monthly rent payment. But if it doesn't, brace yourself for a substantial impact on your lifestyle. And even if that monthly obligation doesn't impinge on your money, it may impinge on your spontaneity. For example, if you get a once-in-a-lifetime chance to spend the summer working on an Alaskan cruise ship, you may find it difficult to take advantage of the opportunity. Unlike a landlord, you can't give a lender 30 days' notice.

Fourth, you must support the twin sister of the mortgage, the down payment. So even if your lender is willing to accept 30 days' notice, you can't go up to Alaska anyway, because all your savings for such frivolities are sunk into the down payment on the house! Similarly, the down payment money is not available for such causes as starting your own business, traveling, or medical emergencies.

Finally, before you sign the marriage certificate, you should be aware of the home's oldest offspring--risk. One risk of home ownership is losing money because the home doesn't appreciate or appreciates very slowly. While this is rare in the Bay Area real estate market, it does happen. Boston is a recent example of how years of spiralling appreciation can be followed by a plummeting real estate market. Secondly, the San Andreas fault is not a myth created to keep seismologists employed. Even if an earthquake doesn't harm you personally, it could destroy your property. If you are renting you simply find another place to live. But if you own, you may never recover financially.

The home's five children--time investment, maintenance, mortgage, down payment, and risk--may grow from ornery brats in the initial years of home ownership into perfect little angels as your income and lifestyle evolves.

If it appears you *should* enter into a marraige contract with a house, next determine whether you *can* pursue real estate ownership. Can you afford to purchase your own living space?

CAN I BUY?

Home Loans

The median price for a home in the Bay Area is $265,000. You perhaps don't have that amount of money sitting around, so you must borrow it. Therefore, to determine whether you can afford to buy a home, you must understand, and even wallow in, the filthy, high-finance world of **Bank Loans.**

Before we examine a typical loan from a bank, let's ease into it with a nontypical loan, to get a feel for the concepts. Let's say you borrow $100 from the bank. The bank lets you keep the $100 for one year. But after one year you must return the full $100. While you have the bank's money, the lender requires 12% interest per year, paid in monthly installments. Since 12% of $100 is $12, you pay the bank $1 per month for one year, then return the $100. This type of loan is called a "one-year, interest-only, fixed-rate loan with a balloon." The "balloon" is the repayment of the principal (the $100) at the end of the loan period.

Prior to the '40s, most loans were balloon-type loans. Every five or ten years the principal would come due (i.e., the balloon had to be paid by the borrower). It is for this reason that so many homes were repossessed during the Great Depression.

With the passage of Regulation Q following World War II, mortgage money was created for prospective home buyers. Regulation Q allowed savings and loan companies to pay 1/4% higher interest than banks. This differential was substantial enough to induce most savers to deposit funds in savings and loan institutions rather than banks. However, Regulation Q stipulated that the savings and loans had to reinvest funds in home loans. Therefore, a great pool of capital flowed into the housing market. The loans made by the savings and loans differed from those made prior to World War II. These new loans were "fully amortized," which means that over their life, the loans are gradually paid off.

Let's now make our $100 one-year loan similar to these post-war loans, namely fully amortized. This gets mathematically intense. However, comprehending the concept is more important than understanding the arithmetic.

In addition to monthly interest payments, a fully amortized loan requires monthly repayment of part of the principal. ("Principal," remember, is another word for "amount borrowed.") In this way, at the end of the loan period, the loan is completely paid off--no more balloon payment is involved. Since part of the principal is paid to the bank every month, the balance of the money owed to the bank decreases every month. Since interest is charged only on the money still owed, the monthly interest payment decreases.

Now suppose that even though the interest payment decreases the monthly payment to the bank remains fixed. Stated as an equation, we have:

interest payment + principal payment =
    fixed monthly payment

The money attributed to principal increases every month as the money attributed to interest decreases. Therefore, the total monthly payment remains fixed.

Figure 1 depicts how the one-year fully amortized loan of $100 evolves over the course of a year and how the loan is completely paid off in 12 equal payments.

Note from the table that the total amount paid to the bank is $106.60. In the case of the balloon-payment loan, the total paid to the bank was $112.00. The fully amortized loan, for a given loan period and a given interest rate, is usually a better deal. The only advantage of the balloon-payment loan is that the monthly payments are lower: $1.00 per month compared to $8.89 per month in this particular case.

Figure 1. Progression of a One-Year Fully Amortized Loan

Annual percentage rate: 12%
Original loan amount: $100
Monthly payment: $8.89
Term: 12 months

Payment #	Interest Payment	Principal Payment	Balance of Loan
1	$1.00	$7.89	$92.11
2	.92	7.97	84.14
3	.84	8.05	76.09
4	.76	8.13	67.96
5	.68	8.21	59.75
6	.60	8.29	51.46
7	.51	8.38	43.08
8	.43	8.46	34.62
9	.35	8.54	26.08
10	.26	8.63	17.45
11	.17	8.72	8.73
12	.08	8.73	0
	$6.60	100.00	

A typical home loan is not $100, but closer to $100,000. A $100,000 fully amortized one-year loan at 12% interest would require monthly mortgage payments of $8,884.88. This is a little steep for most borrowers. But lenders have seen this dilemma and taken mercy upon the masses. Instead of requiring that the loan be fully amortized in one year, they have stretched the repayment period to 30 years. Since the borrower has longer to return the original amount borrowed, the monthly mortgage payments are lower.

As an example, let's examine what happens to the $100 loan if it is converted from a one-year, fully amortized loan to a 30-year fully amortized loan. As the second figure shows, the monthly loan payment goes from $8.89 to $1.03. The loan payments are now nearly equivalent to the interest-only balloon-payment loan. In fact, most of the monthly payment is dedicated to interest in the early years of the loan. Note that the first payment reduces the outstanding balance by only 3 cents. Since, in the initial years of a 30-year loan, your monthly payment is mostly interest, you repay the bank much more money than you originally borrowed. In the present example of $100 at 12% interest, you pay the bank $370.80 over the 30-year period, i.e., $270.80 in interest.

**Figure 2. First Payment of a 30-Year
Fully Amortized Loan**

Annual percentage rate: 12%
Original loan amount: $100
Monthly payment: $1.03
Term: 30 years

Payment #	Interest Payment	Principal Payment	Loan Balance
1	$1.00	$.03	99.97

The House Affordability Equation

Now let's extend these ideas to the actual purchase of a house.

Typically, the money borrowed from the bank covers 80% of the purchase price. The rest of the money must come out of your pocket. This out-of-pocket money is called a "down payment." The down payment plus the financing equal the full price of the house.

A financial institution determines the amount of money it lends you based primarily upon your monthly income. The lender looks only tangentially at the value of the house. It's you, not the house, that makes the monthly payments. Only in foreclosure is the house value of concern to the bank. And the bank doesn't want to foreclose. Foreclosure is a pain in the neck to the bank. The lender greatly prefers a steady flow of monthly mortgage payments from the borrower. For this reason, even if you locate a fabulous deal on a house, don't expect the banker to get as excited as your best friend. The lender still demands that you meet minimum income requirements.

And what are these minimum income requirements? Typically financial institutions require that no more than 28% of your gross monthly income be dedicated to PITI (principal, interest, property taxes, and property insurance.) Furthermore, banks demand that your monthly PITI payments, plus any other long-term debt payments, be no more than 36% of your gross monthly income. These percentage figures are known as "qualifying ratios."

The house you can afford is further influenced by "closing costs," which are the lender's fees, the escrow fees, the title insurance premium, and local taxes. Part Two examines closing costs in more detail.

Clearly, the house price you can afford is influenced by an overwhelming array of variables. Down payment, interest rate, closing costs, property taxes, property insurance, monthly income, and the lender's qualifying ratio must all be accounted for. Figure 3 presents the relationship between these factors as three separate equations. By solving the equations sequentially (plugging the answer from one equation into the next equation), you can estimate the house price you can afford.

Figure 3 makes some assumptions that greatly simplify the equations. First, it assumes that your monthly loan payment is all interest, no principal. Recall that this is essentially true during the initial years of a 30-year loan. Second, it assumes that property tax plus property insurance comprise 20% of your monthly loan payment. This 20% translates into the .80 coefficient of Equation 1. Third, closing costs are estimated at 5% of the loan amount. This is where the .95 fudge factor in Equation 3 originates. As an example, let's determine how much house can be purchased by a family earning the Bay Area median income.

Figure 3. The Affordabilty Equation

Simplifying assumptions:
1. The loan is interest only.
2. The property tax and property insurance are 20% of the monthly loan payment.
3. Closing costs are 20% of the loan amount.

Legend:
M = Monthly loan payments you can afford, according to the lender.
R = Ratio used by lender to qualify borrower; use decimal equivalent (e.g., 28% = .28).
F = Amount the bank will lend you. A more precise value for "F" can be found using a mortgage table.
I = Interest rate on loan; use decimal equivalent.
D = Down payment.

Eq. 1 $M = R \times$ your gross monthly income $\times .80$
Eq. 2 $F = (M \times 12)/I$
Eq. 3 House price you can afford $= D + (F \times .95)$

The median family income in the Bay Area is about $3,700 per month. Assume this typical household has saved up $26,252 for a down payment. (This down payment figure was carefully chosen to equal 20% of the house price, as will be seen.) Assume that the lender's qualifying ratio is 28% and that the interest rate on the loan is 9%. As derived in Figure 4, the house this typical family can afford costs $131,258. Unfortunately for our typical family, the median price for a house in the Bay Area is $265,000--$134,000 beyond what the average family can afford!

If you find this depressing, you are not alone. The National Association of Realtors publishes statistics that quantify just how depressing the housing situation is. Called the "affordability gap," this figure measures the difference between the monthly median income and the monthly income needed to purchase a median-priced home. The affordability gap was worst in 1981, when the median income in the U.S. was less than two-thirds the income required to purchase a median-priced home. Presently, the nationwide annual median income of $35,000 per household is barely enough to purchase the nationwide median-priced home of $95,000.

**Figure 4. Typical Bay Area Household
Affordabilty Calculation**

R   = .28
Monthly income = $3,700
I   = .09
D   = $26,252

Eq. 1   M =   .28 x $3,700 x .80 = $829
Eq. 2   F = $829 x $\frac{12}{.09}$ = $110,533
Eq. 3   House price family can afford =
               $26,252 + ($110,533 x .95) = $131,258

When you plug your own salary and down payment figures into the equation, set the value of R to .28 (28% monthly loan payment to monthly income ratio), and be sure to exclude from your gross monthly income any interest presently earned on the money to be used as a down payment. To determine I, assume a 30-year fixed-rate loan. The interest rate on such a loan can be found in the real estate section of your newspaper or obtained from your local bank.

Figure 5. Amortization Table

Interest:	8%		9%		10%	
Years:	15	30	15	30	15	30
Amount						
1,000	9.56	7.34	10.15	8.05	10.75	8.78
2,000	19.12	14.68	20.29	16.10	21.50	17.56
3,000	28.67	22.02	30.43	24.14	32.24	26.33
4,000	38.23	29.36	40.58	32.19	42.99	35.11
5,000	47.79	36.69	52.72	40.24	53.74	43.88
6,000	57.34	44.03	60.86	48.28	64.48	52.66
7,000	66.90	51.37	71.00	56.33	75.23	61.44
8,000	76.46	58.71	81.15	64.37	85.97	70.21
9,000	86.01	66.04	91.29	72.42	96.72	78.99
10,000	95.57	73.38	101.43	80.47	107.47	87.76
20,000	191.14	146.76	202.86	160.93	214.93	175.52
30,000	286.70	220.13	304.28	241.39	322.39	263.28
40,000	382.27	293.51	405.71	321.85	429.85	351.03
50,000	477.83	366.89	507.14	402.32	537.31	438.79
60,000	573.40	440.26	608.56	482.78	644.77	526.55
70,000	668.96	513.64	709.99	563.24	752.23	614.31
80,000	764.53	587.02	811.42	643.70	859.69	702.06
90,000	860.10	660.40	912.84	724.17	967.15	789.82
100,000	955.66	733.77	1014.27	804.63	1074.61	877.58

If you discover you can barely afford the neighbor's doghouse, then Part Three is for you. Although the Bay Area housing situation is bleak, it is possible for a first-time home buyer to purchase a house. Part Three is dedicated to bridging the affordability gap.

Before leaving the affordability equation, let's examine one final detail. Equation 2 uses the simplifying assumption that the entire monthly mortgage payment (M) is allocated to interest payments. But the mortgage payment of an amortized loan covers not only interest but also principal. So the affordability equation is more accurate if we use an "amortization table" instead of Equation 2. Amortization tables list monthly mortgage payments for any given loan amount, loan period, and interest rate. They are available from libraries, book stores, and title companies. Figure 5 is a section from an amortization table.

Using Figure 5 instead of Equation 2, we discover that the median-income family can qualify for a loan of $103,000, which is indeed close to the $110,533 given by Equation 2 of Figure 4. The details of using the amortization table are shown in Figure 6.

Figure 6. Using the Amortization Table

A Monthly Payment of:	Yields a Loan Amount of:
$804.63	$100,000
+ 24.14	+ 3,000
$828.77	$103,000

The family can afford a monthly loan payment of $829. They are considering a 30-year fully amortized loan at 9% interest. If Figure 5 had a listing close to $829, the loan amount could be read directly from the table. Since it does not, the two-step process of Figure 6 is required.

Tax Implications

The lender doesn't consider your potential tax savings when determining whether you can afford a home loan. On the loan application you state your gross income (i.e., before taxes), so your tax situation is not accounted for. However, when *you* are deciding whether you feel you can afford a house, your tax situation most assuredly should be considered. The interest paid on your home loan may be deducted from your income, thereby reducing your income tax. Therefore, your home may be a fantastic tax as well as physical shelter. Deduction of interest paid on the mortgage of a principal residence is one of the few tax write-offs left untouched by the recent tax overhaul.

**Figure 7. Tax Rate Schedule
for 1989**

| | Your tax is | | |
If your adjusted gross income is	Base:	Plus:	Of amount over:
Single:			
$ 0 - 18,550	$ 0	11%	$ 0
$ 18,551 - 44,900	$ 2,782	28%	$ 18,850
$ 44,901 - 93,130	$ 10,160	33%	$ 44,900
Married:			
$ 0 - 30,950	$ 0	15%	$ 0
$ 30,951 - 74,850	$ 4,642	28%	$ 30,950
$ 74,851 - 155,320	$ 16,934	33%	$ 74,850

Standard deduction for single: $3,100
Standard deduction for married: $5,200
Personal exemption: $2,000

The tax schedule and personal exemption rates for 1989 are shown in Figure 7. Let's take an example to see how your mortgage can reduce your income tax.

Batya and Peter, a married couple, made $56,000 in
1989. As renters they are allowed the $4,000 personal
exemption and the $5,200 standard deduction, with a
resulting taxable income of $46,800. Their federal tax
liability is therefore $9,080. However, Batya and Peter
own their own home and in 1989 paid $16,000 on their
home loan. For simplicity, assume the $16,000 is all
interest. Remember that in actuality it's part interest
payment and part principal payment. The principal is not
tax deductible. Instead of taking the standard deduction,
they itemize their deductions, and their federal tax
liability reduces to $5,356. The tax savings is therefore
$3,724 or about 23% of the $16,000. Figure 8 details the
calculations.

When a more rigorous analysis is done that includes
state tax savings, their total tax savings due to home
ownership is found to be $4,870 or 30% of the $16,000
mortgage! The tax considerations effectively reduce a
monthly house payment of $1,333 to $927. You can see
why there is a public outcry any time Congress attempts
to dismantle this tax-saving legislation.

Figure 8. Federal Income Tax

	Renter	Owner
Income	$56,000	$56,000
Personal Exemption	4,000	4,000
Standard Deduction	5,200	0
Property Tax	0	2,500
Mortgage Payments	0	16,000
Taxable Income	$46,800	$33,500
Tax	$ 9,080	$ 5,356
Difference in favor of owning:		$3,724

For a rough estimate of tax savings, simply look up
your income tax bracket in the "Tax Rate Schedule" from
Figure 7. For example, in the case of Batya and Peter,
married taxpayers in 1989 earning $56,000 annually are

in the 28% tax bracket. This is close to the 30% found upon detailed analysis.

Renting Versus Owning

These tax benefits, in conjunction with other considerations, make home ownership less costly than it would appear initially. For example, Batya and Peter may shudder at the thought of a $1,333-per-month mortgage payment. However, an after-tax mortgage payment of $927 per month may approximate what they would have paid in rent. Were they to base the rent-versus-own decision entirely upon financial considerations, however, they must take into account much more than tax differences. Housing appreciation, closing costs, rental inflation, home-loan interest rates, realtor's commission, utilities, tax rate changes, savings-account interest rates, maintenance costs, property tax, and insurance premiums must all be considered in comparing the cost of renting a home to the cost of buying a home. But the question "Does it pay to own?" is important enough that we should roll up our sleeves and tackle it. By making certain assumptions we can greatly simplify our task.

We will compare Batya and Peter's housing costs for five years. In one case they rent for five years and invest the money they would have used for the down payment and the closing costs. In the other case they use their savings as a down payment on a house, live in the house for five years, and then sell.

Let's investigate owning first, and base our analysis on these assumptions: The house costs $190,000. Batya and Peter divide their $46,000 savings between the closing costs ($8,000) and the down payment ($38,000). They obtain a 30-year fixed-rate loan of $152,000 to cover the remainder of the house price. The mortgage payments are $16,000 per year (thus our tax analysis done earlier holds true). Their mortgage payments remain fixed over the five-year period. The fraction of the mortgage payment allocated to interest decreases slightly every year, and therefore their tax deduction for mortgage interest will likewise decrease. However, for tax purposes we assume the entire $16,000 annual mortgage payment is all interest. Therefore, they realize the $3,724 tax savings (as derived earlier) for every year of home ownership. Assume that the housing costs outlined in Figure 9 rise with inflation at an annual rate of 5% (except property tax, which rises at a maximum rate of 2% under Proposition 13). The average annual housing appreciation in the Bay Area over the past ten years has been about 11%, and that figure is used in our analysis.

**Figure 9. Housing Costs in Addition to
Mortgage Payments***

Property Tax	Hazard Ins.	Maint. & Repairs	Utilities	PMI
1.3%	.5%	1.5%	1.0%	.4%

*Costs are expressed as a percentage of house price. Insurance, maintenance, and utilities rise with inflation over the years. Property tax rises no more than 2% per year. PMI remains fixed over the years.

Figure 10 details the calculations. After living in the home for five years and then selling, their total profit is $53,400. The income tax liability Batya and Peter will encounter upon selling the home has been ignored, because they may defer the tax by purchasing another residence within 24 months.

If they rent, we're assuming they can invest the $46,000 they used for the down payment and closing costs at 10% interest. They are taxed on this extra income. Therefore, to make the comparison accurate, we assume they withdraw part of the interest every year to pay the extra income tax the interest creates. The effective interest is therefore 7%. It is estimated that a $190,000 home could be rented for $900 per month. Their rental cost is therefore $10,800 the first year and increases by 5% every year. Their investment after five years minus their rental costs results in a positive cash flow of $4,840 over the five-year period. So the total difference between home ownership and renting is $48,560 in favor of home ownership. Put another way, home ownership saved them about $10,000 every year.

So should Batya and Peter buy a house or rent? Based on the assumptions outlined above, the figures suggest they should buy. But if we alter any one of the assumptions upon which this analysis is based, the answer to the above question may change dramatically. Many of these assumptions require predicting the future. which is usually difficult to do (and predicting housing appreciation is nearly impossible).

I must emphasize that renting a home instead of buying is not the worst financial catastrophe in the world. If, upon finishing this book, you determine that renting is your only option, it doesn't mean you are doomed to economic disaster. In the present economy of moderate interest rates and steep home prices, *home ownership is not a financial panacea.* However, there are ethereal benefits to owning that defy economic analysis. What is it worth to be able to dig up the yard and plant a garden, or put nail holes in the wall, or add a darkroom? Upon settling into my own home, I found a sense of roots, of belonging, that had eluded me during my many years as a renter. Furthermore, I began to open my home to friends and relatives in a way I had never done as a renter, probably because I had never felt it was *my* home to open.

If the economic analysis in Batya and Peter's case indicated that renting and owning were financially comparable, I would advise them to buy a home. Since the figures in fact suggest that they may be $48,000 ahead if they buy, I would strongly urge them to go for it! To determine if owning makes financial sense for you, reference 155 prepares renting versus owning computerized analyses.

Figure 10. Housing Costs

Assumptions: Married couple earns $56,000 per year. They are comparing renting and keeping their $46,000 in savings (earning after tax interest of 7%) to investing the $46,000 in a house. The home they are considering costs $190,000, with closing costs of $8,000 on a loan of $152,000. Their rent is $900 per month.

	Total After Five Years	Summary
Own		
Credits		
House value	$320,161	
Tax Savings	18,620	
		+ 338,781
Debits		
Loan balance	146,832	
Interest payments	74,832	
Property tax	13,010	
Property insurance	5,249	
Maintenance	15,748	
Utilities	10,500	
		- 266,171
Realtor's commission		- 19,210
Owner's total after five years		+ 53,400
Rent		
Credits		
Investment	64,517	+ 64,517
Debits		
Annual rent	59,677	- 59,677
Renter's total after five years		+ 4,840

PART TWO

HOUSE HUNTING AND PURCHASE OFFERS

This section examines the nuts and bolts of house hunting and purchase offers. Searching for a house, as one might expect, is both fun and nerve wracking. By being prepared and keeping a few principles in mind, one can accentuate the former and reduce the latter.

DO YOUR HOMEWORK!

The importance of arming yourself with real estate basics before jumping into the trenches cannot be over-emphasized. Luckily this is not difficult to do, and plenty of resources are available to help you through real estate boot camp. For example, the real estate section of your local newspaper is bursting with valuable information. Just how valuable varies from one newspaper to another. Figure 11 rates several San Francisco Bay Area papers.

Figure 11. San Francisco Bay Area Newspapers

Newspaper	Real Estate Section		Mortgage Survey		
	Day	Quality[1]	Day	Section	Source[2]
Contra Costa Times	Sun.	Good	Sun.	R.E.	R/N
S.F. Chron./Exam.	Sun.	Great	Sun.	R.E.	MMW
S.F. Chronicle	none		Mon.	Bus.	Note[3]
San Jose Mercury	Sat.	Great	Mon.	Bus.	R/N
Tribune (East Bay)	Sun.	Fair	Sun.	R.E.	R/N
Pen. Times Tribune	Sat.	Fair	Sat.	R.E.	R/N
Sacramento Bee	Sat./Sun.	Good	Sun.	R.E.	Note[3]
Sacramento Union	Sat./Sun.	Great	Sat./Sun.	R.E.	Note[3]
Inter-City Express	Note[4]	Great	Fri.	R.E.	R/N

Notes:
1. Fair: Mostly press releases. Few columnists.
   Good: Informative articles, some columnists.
   Great: Informative articles, many columnists, seminar announcements, etc.
2. R/N: Real/Net. Rates listed in the newspaper are a sampling from their Bay Area survey, and are not necessarily the best offerings. See Reference 97.
   MMW: Mortgage Market Weekly. Publishes in the newspaper the best rates from their survey. Complete survey is not available to the public.
3. Newspaper conducts its own survey every week.
4. Newspaper is dedicated to real estate, published Monday-Friday. See Reference 13.

Go to the library and read real estate sections from the past three months. While you're there, check the back issues of *California Real Estate* magazine. Locate other magazine articles on real estate, housing finance, house buying, and mortgages by looking up these headings in the library's "Index of Periodicals." Having done this, check out a book on real estate. Inundate yourself! You have not done enough research until Fannie Mae and Allen Greenspan are haunting your dreams!

In conjunction with this reading, the serious buyer may also consider taking a short course or seminar on real estate. Seminars are listed in the real estate section of the paper. The resource section at the end of this book also lists many educational sources on real estate.

Having mastered the basic concepts, it is time to confront the most terrifying question of your life. With "Ride of the Valkyrie" blaring on the stereo, look into a mirror and ask yourself, "What sort of house do I want?" You save yourself tremendous frustration and time by knowing what you want *before* hitting the streets.

To determine what you want, begin by choosing a house-hunting price range. You have already solved the affordability equation assuming 30-year fixed-rate financing. This is the lower end of your price range. Now return to Figure 3 and plug in an interest rate 2% lower than the fixed-rate loan. This gives your upper price limit. (This 2% figure will be discussed in Part 3.)

Continuing your sojourn of self-reflection, determine the features you want in a living environment. This exercise is not only valuable but can be fun as well! Figure 12 suggests some questions you should consider, but only scratches the surface of the many issues you might explore. I encourage you to modify and expand on Figure 12 to meet your own needs. Having decided on the features you want in a living environment, establish priorities by dividing the features into three categories: "must have," "should have," and "would like to have." Shoot for a house that includes most of your "would like to have" characteristics, and don't bother looking at homes that don't meet your "must have" criteria. Give this stage of your homework careful consideration. Nothing is more distressing than buying a house only to realize one year later that it isn't really what you want!

Figure 12. House Hunter's Checklist

Your Life:
*   Will your family size change while in the home?
*   Is it important to live near friends or relatives?
*   Are you willing to invest time into remodeling or repair?
*   Are you planning a career change soon that might involve relocating?
*   Do you spend a lot of time at home? Indoors or out?
*   What climate and environment do you prefer?
*   What activities are important to you (for example: theater, skiing, horseback riding, dining, backpacking, music)? How will home ownership impact these activities?
*   Do you like to entertain guests in your home?
*   If you are buying the property with a partner, how are your needs and desires different? How are they similar? Can you compromise?
*   Are you willing to accept the financial hardships home ownership may initially bring?
*   What sacrifices are you willing to make for home ownership? Which are you not willing to make?

Your Community:
*   Would you like an urban, suburban, or rural area?
*   Is school quality important to you?
*   Do you have preferences regarding the predominant race, religion, and age group?
*   Would you like to derive a sense of community from your neighborhood? Would you like neighbors who know each other and socialize?
*   Must there be playmates for your children?
*   Are local gathering areas like parks, community centers, or cafes a consideration?
*   Would you like a strictly residential neighborhood?

* How much time are you willing to spend commuting to work?
* Is traffic noise or other noise a consideration?
* Is it important to live in a low crime area?
* Would you like to own the nicest home on the block? Would you feel bad if you owned the worst?
* Is it important that the neighborhood homes be well maintained?
* Must you be near shopping centers, schools, child care facilities, and public transportation?
* Would you prefer an old established neighborhood or a relatively new one?

Your Home:
* What style do you want (Victorian, ranch, Cape Cod, modern)?
* Would you mind a fixer-upper?
* How many bedrooms do you need? How many bathrooms?
* Do you need a workshop? A garage? A yard? A fireplace? A large kitchen? A lot of storage space?
* Is lots of sun important? How about a view?
* Must the electrical system support future additions?
* Would you like an extra room or in-law apartment you can rent out?
* Should your home be accessible to the elderly or disabled?

REAL ESTATE AGENTS

Okay, let's assume that you have poured over a nauseating quantity of real estate information, that you have determined your house-hunting price range, and that you have determined your housing needs and desires. You feel confident with your own knowledge of real estate. Now it is time to meet your very first real estate agent.

To get your feet wet, grab the Saturday or Sunday real estate section of the paper and look for "Sunday

Open House" advertisements. Drive around, see what's out there. Go to some snazzy areas. Try the complimentary white wine and brie. Have fun!

Most open houses have flyers available that list details of the layout of the house, lot size, seller's name, age of the house, present financing, seller's asking price, and so forth. If there is a real estate agent involved, engage him or her in conversation. Read the flyer and ask questions about anything you have trouble understanding.

Real estate agents are a special breed of human, and you should approach them fully aware of their strengths and weaknesses. Unfortunately, agents can be dangerous. They are tampering with extremely serious items-- namely, vast sums of your money and your time. For most people the purchase of a house is the largest financial commitment they make in their lives. Many real estate agents lack both the training and the mind set to give a home purchase the educated scrutiny and serious attention it deserves.

When dealing with real estate agents, remember this simple fact: They are not there to help you, they are there to sell you something. If you want help, you're going to have to get it yourself.

It is not imperative that an agent be used in executing a home purchase. However, in your housing search you are sure to encounter them. A good real estate agent can be a real blessing and a vital component to a successful home search. Just be certain that, in the end, you rely on your own knowledge and judgment.

Real estate agents are licensed by the state upon successful completion of a few classes in real estate. They make their living from commissions on property they sell. These commissions, which are paid by the sellers, are typically 6 or 7% of the sales price.

A seller lists a property with a real estate agent for two reasons. The first is to take advantage of the training and experience of the agent. This training and experience will hopefully result in a better sales presentation and a well-prepared sales agreement. The second reason is that by listing with a real estate agent, the seller's property is described in a "multiple-listing" book.

A buyer goes to a real estate agent for similar reasons: the agent's training and experience, and the agent's access to information on an enormous number of houses via the multiple-listing book. This book, which is published weekly by the local Board of Realtors, is a catalog of properties for sale by real estate agents in an area. To a buyer, this multiple-listing book is extremely handy. It carries photos of the houses for sale in the area, along with pertinent information on sales price, financing, house size, and so on. The multiple-listing book also documents the actual selling price of local houses. This is helpful in determining true property values (as opposed to asking prices). The multiple-listing service does not list for-sale-by-owner houses.

If you purchase a home listed by your agent, then the entire sales commission goes to your agent. If your real estate agent sells you a home listed by another agent, then the two agents split the commission.

Unlike the arrangement between the seller and seller's agent, there is no formal agreement between a buyer and an agent. A buyer may use many realtors in a housing search. However, since all agents in any given area have access to the same multiple-listing service, there is little advantage in working with more than one agent. In fact, if you work exclusively with one agent, the agent is likely to be much more dedicated and willing to invest time and energy to your search.

How do you find an agent, if you want one? You encounter many agents simply by attending open houses and calling upon homes advertised in the paper. If, in so doing, you discover an agent with whom you feel comfortable, tell that agent you would like to work exclusively with him or her.

In one multiple-listing area I found an agent with whom I hit it off immediately. She had a funky car (which actually died while we were out in the country, forcing us to hitchhike back to town) and she was able to accept the fact that I was on a budget. Many agents tried to talk me into something more expensive, saying that my budget was not realistic. I agreed to work exclusively with her. If I saw a house advertised in the paper, I would not call the listing agent directly. I would call my agent, and she in turn would phone the listing agent. If a sale eventually evolved, she would get half the commission. In exchange for always including her in any potential sale, she dedicated a lot of time and energy to my housing search.

Remember that if an agent shows you a house, the seller is obligated under contract to sell to you only through that agent. Some contracts are written so that even after the listing expires (one to three months), the seller is still forbidden to sell to you directly if the house was originally shown to you by an agent.

Some people are hesitant to buy a house without involving an agent, so they steer clear of for-sale-by-owner homes. However, if the contract and financing are simple, and you have done enough study and research, you should be able to write the sales contract yourself. If the deal is complicated, then a real estate attorney will probably be required to help with the contract anyway, with or without a real estate agent. So, provided you have done your homework, you should have no problem executing a sales agreement without a real estate agent, if you need to.

Be aware that as a buyer, you may not save any money by purchasing a for-sale-by-owner property. The same house being sold without a real estate agent may be lower in price by 6 or 7% but, more likely, the seller may ask the same price and simply pocket the extra money. Sellers, going through the headache of marketing their own home, are probably doing it to save the real estate commission for themselves, not for their buyer!

When a home is placed in the multiple-listing service catalog, a "unilateral offer of subagency" is automatically made to all other agents showing the home. Therefore, unless specified otherwise, "your" agent is actually a subagent of the seller's agent, and under law must represent the best interests of the seller. Your agent assists you in the purchase of a home in the same way a car salesperson assists you in the purchase of a car. The salesperson would not confide in you all the negative features of a car, nor would you confide in the salesperson your willingness to increase your purchase price. The same attitude applies in your relationship with your real estate agent.

If you have done your homework, and approach your agent fully aware that anything you say may reach the ears of the seller, then it does not matter that the agent actually represents the interest of the seller, because you are not relying on your agent to do your thinking for you.

Figure 13. Declaration Regarding Real Estate Agency Relationship
(This is a section of the disclosure form)

_____ is the agent of (check one):
_____ The buyer exclusively; or
_____ The seller exclusively; or
_____ Both the buyer and seller

Confirmed and acknowledged.
Seller _____ Date _____
Buyer _____ Date _____
Agent _____ Date _____

Every agent you talk to will tell you the "car dealer" relationship between buyer and agent is a thing of the past because of the "agency disclosure law" recently implemented in California, which requires agents to divulge in writing just who they represent. They do this by filling out and signing the state-mandated form shown in Figure 13. Recall that agents showing properties from the multiple-listing service are to represent the best interests of the seller unless the "offer of subagency" is specifically declined. Nearly every agent in the Bay Area checks the box on the disclosure form stating that he or she represents the buyer. In so doing the agent declines the offer of subagency, choosing instead to represent the best interests of the buyer. However, local brokers have told me that regardless of which box is checked on the disclosure form, many agents coming to them with offers from buyers still act as if they represent the seller. Agents, supposedly representing the best interests of the buyer, still disclose to the listing agent compromising information about their "client." For eighty years the real estate industry has represented the best interests of the seller, and it will take more than checking a box on a form to change that attitude. Therefore, I advise that you maintain a "car dealer" attitude toward your agent. You may find an agent who appreciates the seriousness of indicating on the agency disclosure statement that he or she is looking out for your best interests. But until you are sure, caution is suggested.

For further information on real estate agents and representation, see references 56 through 59.

THE SEARCH IS ON!

There are a few tricks to ferreting out exceptional deals when hunting for a home. The most important axiom of bargain hunting is: Buy the cheapest house in a good neighborhood, never the nicest house in a bad neighborhood. Why? Because homes in a bad neighborhood, even the best homes, appreciate in value much more slowly than homes in a good neighborhood. A "bad" neighborhood is defined as one with a high crime rate and an undesirable school district. The glaring exception to this axiom is an "up-and-coming" neighborhood, where residents are actively rejuvenating their homes and environment, perhaps with the assistance of the local government's redevelopment department.

One bargain-hunting method is to locate a motivated seller. For example, homes listed in the paper in the middle of the week indicate a more anxious seller than those listed only on the weekend. Determine why the seller is selling. If the owner is being forced to sell because of a divorce or job change, for example, she or he is more apt to wheel and deal than if there are no precipitating circumstances.

Another bargain-hunting technique is to limit your competition. Don't go out house hunting on a picture-perfect spring day, when both birds and prices are soaring. Wait for a dismal streak of weather. With most home buyers huddled by the fireplace, you should be out splashing the pavement. Also, the papers are filled with homes for sale during November and December, but most prospective buyers are preoccupied with the holidays. A perfect time for a sneak attack. Another technique for limiting your competition is to buy the property before it is placed on the market. Part Three explores this avenue.

A low sales price is only half the bargain-hunting story. A home may have an average price tag yet carry exceptional financing, making it a bargain deal. Financing bargains are investigated in Part Three.

Upon locating a house you're interested in, don your Sherlock Holmes cap and prepare to sleuth. It's time to investigate the home thoroughly and determine if you really want to buy it. If other potential buyers are following close on your heels, make your purchase offer immediately, but make it contingent upon the results of your research. However, if the home won't be stolen from beneath your feet, then take the time to research the house before making a purchase offer. This way you can consider the results of your research when deciding how much to offer. To prevent unnecessary expense, postpone any inspections that cost money until after the offer is accepted.

A wealth of information on any given property resides in the crypts of your local city and county government. To begin your sleuthing, visit the city's building department and department of public works. At each department ask to see the file on the property. These files reveal everything from recent additions to the house to problems with the sewer system. While you're there, drop by the planning and zoning department to ask about flooding, erosion, streets destined for expansion, fault lines, brush fire hazards, landfill, and any planned industry or apartment complexes. Also ask about the policy on variances; if they are granted easily and often, zoning laws have little meaning.

After the check at the city, visit the school(s) your children will attend. The school district office or local Board of Realtors can usually refer you to a school-by-school comparison of student tests. Even if you have no children, the school district plays an important role in the resale value of the home. References 134 and 137 thoroughly investigate San Francisco Bay Area school rankings.

In addition, the crime rate in the neighborhood influences both the resale value of the home and your happiness while living there. The local police department can give you crime statistics for any given area.

Insurance agents make their living by knowing details about neighborhoods. Tell your agent where you are thinking of buying. Ask if your car insurance premium will go up or down and inquire about the cost of fire insurance on the home. Get an insurance agent talking and you will learn more than you ever hoped to know about an area.

When you reach the point of making an offer on a house, you should have done enough hunting that you instinctively know the approximate value of the house. But if you need a "Bluebook" comparison, ask your agent to show you the multiple listing's "cumulative index" for the area. This index outlines asking price, selling price, number of days on the market, and other details about recently sold homes. For further peace of mind, you may ask the seller to show you any recent appraisals of the house.

If you would like to become completely depressed, the price the *seller* paid for the home may be determined from the local transfer tax, available at the county recorder's office. Keep in mind that any loans the seller has assumed are not reflected in the transfer tax. Real estate agents and title companies may also be able to provide information on the seller's purchase price.

A "title report" states the legal owner of the house, as well as which bank, if any, holds the loan on the house. The title report may also list other liens and encumbrances against the property. You should ask to see a copy of the title report early in the buying process. Title reports will be discussed later in greater detail.

A car buyer wouldn't purchase a car without first taking it for a test drive. However, the same concept has yet to be accepted by the real estate industry. If the house is vacant, demand that it pass a 24-hour test drive. Move in for a day. Or, if the home is occupied, spend as much time in the home as you can. It is time well spent should you discover that the street doubles as a short cut for rush-hour traffic, or that the backyard doubles as a crack den for neighborhood kids. As you spend time in the home, imagine waking up in the seller's bedroom, taking your morning shower in the seller's bathroom, going outside and saying good morning to the seller's neighbor. How does it feel? Spending excessive time in your potential home is frowned upon by both real estate agents and sellers. However, this is the largest purchase you may ever make. Therefore, in your offer request permission for some unhurried time in the house.

While you have the house out for a test drive, you might as well open up the hood and really get your hands dirty. You can teach yourself the basics of inspecting a house by studying any of the many how-to house inspection books. I recommend the excellent book by George Hoffman, *How to Inspect a House* (reference 125).

If the lender feels it is warranted, a "termite report" may be required before a loan is issued. These reports warn of termite damage, dry rot, and other structural problems. The lender may require that repairs be made before the loan is granted. If a termite report has been done within the last two years, you may order a copy of the report from reference 132.

Even if the lender doesn't require a termite report, you may want to hire a professional housing inspector to confirm your own judgments of the home. Listed under "Building Inspection Services" in the Yellow Pages, a housing inspector provides a detailed written analysis on the soundness of the home. The fee of about $250 is usually paid by the buyer.

Unlike termite inspection companies, building inspectors are not licensed in California. However, if they belong to an inspector's professional organization, then they have agreed to follow the standards of practice of the organization. The main professional organization in California is the American Society of Home Inspectors. Contact reference 128 for a listing of members.

A growing number of new home builders prohibit independent professional inspections of their homes until the home is purchased by the buyer, citing insurance liability as the reason. However, you may rightfully ask yourself what the builder has to hide from the scrutiny of a professional inspector. Ask about the builder's independent inspection policy prior to signing a contract. Current residents of the housing complex are an equally valuable resource. If the development is still under construction, visit other housing projects the builder has recently completed. Ask residents about the quality of construction and about the developer's responsiveness to complaints.

In addition to an inspection, a "home warranty" can provide further peace of mind. These one-year warranties, available from reference 126, cover malfunctions due to normal wear and tear in wiring, plumbing, built-in appliances, water heater, and furnace. The buyer typically pays the premium of about $350.

Home warranties are also available on new homes. New home warranties became more uniform in 1974 with the creation of the Home Owners Warranty (HOW) Corporation. Under HOW, new homes are protected against cosmetic, utility, and structural defects for two years by the builder, and against structural defects for the next eight years by HOW. If during the first two years the builder either cannot or will not respond to claims by the buyer, the HOW program honors the builder's obligation. The HOW premiums are paid by the builder. See references 130 and 131.

PURCHASE OFFERS AND THE LAW

There are serious legal implications to making a purchase offer on a house. The purchase offer must be carefully worded to avoid costly mistakes. Real estate purchase forms ease some of the anxiety of making serious legal errors. These forms, which are not standardized, can be obtained from reference 3, reference 6, or the local Board of Realtors. At the top of the form you will find the words **"This Is More Than a Receipt for Money. This Is a Legally Binding Contract. Read It Carefully."** This phrase never failed to make my hands sweaty.

In the body of the contract the terms of the sale are spelled out. The contract outlines the down payment, the financing, and any special conditions of the sale.

If the offer is accepted by the seller, a deposit called "earnest money" is given to a title company. The amount is not set by law but is typically less than 1% of the sales price. Since this can be a substantial sum it is imperative to describe carefully the conditions under which the earnest money is returned. If the purchase actually transpires, the deposit is applied toward the down payment.

Contingency clauses stipulate conditions under which the contract becomes null and void and the earnest money is returned to the buyer. One common clause is the inspection contingency: "This offer contingent upon buyer's or his/her representative's complete inspection and approval of the property." This is the "cold-feet" escape clause. If your personal inspection reveals unacceptable problems with the home (for example, the neighbor's mutant poodle dog practices primal yipping exercises at three o'clock in the morning) then the home does not pass your inspection and the contract becomes null and void. Likewise, if the professional inspection reveals unacceptable flaws, then you do not waive the inspection contingency and you may thereby get out of a legally binding contract. If the inspections reveal problems, yet you still want to buy the home, you have three options. You can accept the problems, ask the seller to fix the problems, or lower your offer to compensate for the unfavorable inspection.

A second common contingency involves financing. For example, the clause might read: "This offer contingent upon buyer and property qualifying for a new 30-year first mortgage of at least $160,000, with a fixed interest rate less than 10%, and with a loan fee not to exceed 1.5 points." If such a loan proves to be unavailable, you can either accept the best available terms or get the deposit refunded.

Stipulate a "day of closing walk through" as the final contingency to be waived. This ensures that when ownership is transferred to you the house is in acceptable condition, and any amenities that were to be included in the sale, such as a built-in stereo or drapes, are indeed still there.

I made eight purchase offers in my two-year search for property. In all eight cases the offers were ultimately accepted by the sellers, and I backed out of every deal except one. I never once had to forfeit my deposit money, thanks to carefully worded escape clauses.

One final note on the content of these contracts. For every action to be taken by the seller or buyer, specify a reasonable time limit, such as five working days.

HAGGLING

As in purchasing a used car, negotiating is an accepted practice in home buying. A few anecdotes from my own experience will serve as examples of what to expect in the bartering process. Although the majority of my offers were for land, the concepts hold for house buying as well. Hopefully, the spirit of adventure, even playfulness, will come through. It is a rare experience to wheel and deal with such large numbers. Be careful, but enjoy it!

I found some land that was a house builder's dream. It was a one-acre plot that abutted 600 acres of public land, with few other houses around. The land sloped gently upward, leveling off into a field nestled among oak trees. And it was priced $20,000 below comparable lots in the area. I nearly died.

The real estate agent assured me that since there was a house right across the street, all the utilities were easily accessible. I decided to double check. Just as I suggested to you earlier, I ravaged the city and county files. I then called the gas and electric company, the sewer district, the telephone company, the sanitation company, and the water district. Everything checked out fine except at the water district. The district representative explained that the border of the water district was defined by the road on which the land was located. Yes, the house across the street had water, and no, I couldn't have any of it. Bringing water to the property would involve hooking onto the water main one mile away, at an estimated cost of $40,000. I dropped the land, and the agent, like a hot potato.

This brings up the issue of "disclosure" on the part of real estate agents and sellers. Consumer protection laws have rendered the old adage "Let the buyer beware" almost obsolete. Recent California legislation requires realty agents and sellers to disclose all *known* defects by completing a "Real Estate Transfer Disclosure Statement." This also applies to property sold "as is." You should request this disclosure document in for-sale-by-owner transactions as well. If, after purchasing the property, you discover an undisclosed defect, you must prove that the agent or seller knew about the defect to get them to pay for damages. This can be difficult. Therefore, to avoid costly mistakes, do your homework.

In the case just mentioned, my preliminary research revealed such a horrendous problem that no purchase offer was made. However, in other cases, any problem discovered in the preliminary research simply became a consideration in the amount offered.

For example, one wooded lot I found in the hills had been pregraded for a driveway and an area had been leveled off for a foundation. A beautiful stream ran through the property, which had a view of an East Bay regional park. Once again, I nearly died. And once again, I did my research.

This time, when I inquired about the property at the department of public works, the man at the counter just laughed, and presented me with a file that was about three inches thick. In wading through the paperwork, I discovered that the grading had been done illegally, was not up to city code, and was causing the surrounding hillside to erode and slide into the houses down the hill. In addition, the beautiful stream would have to be diverted through a cement pipe before a house could be built. I decided to pursue the lot anyway, making my offer contingent upon inspection by a soils and foundation engineer. In the purchase offer, which was far below the asking price, I stated that I was aware of these various city code violations. This statement was included more for its psychological impact than its legal implications.

My offer was rejected. A counter offer was made by the seller, with a three-day time limit on my acceptance or rejection. I felt the price they were asking in the counter offer was too high, and I immediately rejected it. However, I instructed my real estate agent not to inform the seller or their agent of my decision. I wanted the three-day time limit to expire and then have them come to us.

On the third day, as expected, the seller's realty agent called my agent. My agent casually explained that the seller's counter was unacceptable and that his client was looking at other properties. The first part was true; the second part wasn't. I really wanted that lot.

The ploy got the desired result. Within the hour the seller's agent had called back three times and the sellers had called twice. They said I should make a new offer.

Now things were getting fun. I made a new offer, only slightly different from my first offer. Since I was starting to feel cavalier, I included the statement, "This is the buyer's final offer. No counter offer will be considered." The sellers accepted immediately. The engineer's report was very unfavorable, so I eventually backed out of the deal.

The property I ultimately purchased went through several iterations of offers and counter offers. The land was on the market for $60,000. From county records I determined that the seller had paid very little for the lot only a few years back. The lot was for sale by the owner and the owner was not actively advertising it. Therefore, my negotiating tactic was based on using time to my advantage.

I presented my offer of $45,000, including $5,000 down. The seller countered with $50,000, including $20,000 down. I said that was impossible and stopped pursuing it, at least in the seller's eyes.

I then played a waiting game. I somehow *knew* this was the land for me. Furthermore, I had been looking at property constantly for two years and was growing weary. However, I wanted to create the appearance of being disinterested, in the hope that the seller would feel some regret that the sale had been lost and therefore become more willing to accept my terms. Every day that passed I wanted to phone the seller with a new offer. I was afraid someone else might buy the land. Furthermore, I wasn't really confident my ploy would work. But I waited--for two months.

I increased my offer to $50,000, with $10,000 down. Incidentally, I decreased the interest rate of the note to the seller, so the total money paid to the seller was equal to my original offer--it just *looked* like more money on paper. The seller accepted immediately. Whether waiting had actually had an impact on the attitude of the seller I'll never know, but the end result was what I wanted.

Notice that there is a common thread running through all these anecdotes. In every case I did thorough research. Not only did this research yield more favorable purchase agreements, but occasionally prevented disastrous mistakes. And in every case I didn't get caught up in the heat of offers and counter offers, which, believe me, can become exciting. My attitude would have been strikingly different had these been highly desirable properties with potential buyers clambering over me to get at them. But regardless of how desirable a house *appears*, never, ever fail to do exhaustive research. Appearances can deceive.

The frantic Bay Area real estate market has received enormous media attention. Terrifying stories of homes selling hours after being put on the market for $10,000 above asking price have made for some trigger-happy home buyers. While the anecdotal legends are true, in the aggregate, Bay Area homes sell *below* asking price and in weeks, not hours. Although the Bay Area market can be more intense than the rest of the nation, statistics indicate that the horror stories are the exception, not the rule.

AFTER THE PURCHASE OFFER . . .

When an offer is made the deposit is held in "escrow" by a "title company." Let's examine these terms more closely.

Remember as a kid how your brother would grab one of your Lincoln Logs and not give it back? After a few times you learned that the solution to the problem was to grab his bag of marbles and hold it hostage. After sufficient screaming, crying, and physical abuse, you both would say, "Okay, let the baby have his toy." But, of course, you didn't simply return the items in question. There was always the possibility the brat would grab his marbles and ditch you and never return your Lincoln Log.

The solution to the problem was to render arbitration to an impartial third party--Mom. You would each hand the ransomed items to Mom and she would execute the exchange. And she was happy to do it. Why? Because she knew it was preparing you for what you would encounter later in life: escrow.

Escrow is a system in which an impartial third party acts as agent for both seller and buyer, or for both borrower and lender. The third party carries out instructions, delivers papers and documents, and disburses funds. For this service the escrow company charges a fee of around $250, although it varies with the purchase price.

Now, returning to the sibling rivalry, let's say you steal your brother's bag of marbles, yet it doesn't have the desired effect. Your brother doesn't seem to care and confiscates your entire Legos collection to demonstrate his animosity. You later discover the reason for his defiant attitude: The marbles do not belong to your brother, but are borrowed from his best friend. Had you known then what you're about to learn now, you would have demanded that a title search be done before pillaging your brother's stash.

"Title" is the record of all parties holding a lien or easement on the house. A house held as collateral for a loan is said to have a "lien" against it. An "easement" is recorded against the house if another party may enter the property from time to time. For example, a neighbor may need to cross the property to get to his home, or a utility company may need to enter the property to access a public utility. All of this is recorded on a title report, which is provided by a title insurance company. The title company may also act as the escrow agent. Not only does the company provide the report, but it also guarantees the accuracy of the report with "title insurance." For example, if after the purchase the IRS attempts to foreclose on you to satisfy a $10,000 federal income tax lien against the seller, the title insurance company will settle the claim. The one-time insurance premium costs $300 to $500, depending on the home price. Never buy property without obtaining a title report and title insurance.

The most common type of title insurance is a lender's policy, which insures the mortgage lender against losses due to title defects. An American Land Title Association (ALTA) policy is another name for a lender's policy. In addition to an ALTA policy, insist on an "owner's policy" to guard your own equity against losses arising from title disputes. Most buyers aren't told of this second policy.

Incidentally, examine the title carefully. Since this is an important legal document, one would think the title company would go to great pains to make it immaculate. However, upon studying the one I was issued before purchase, I discovered my name was spelled wrong, the wrong county was specified, and the lot numbers were incorrect.

I have alluded to a "deed of trust" without fully explaining what it is. Back to the sibling dispute. Your mom finally gets wise and sends your creepy brother to summer camp. He asks to borrow your Swiss Army knife, promising to return it. You say, "No way, Buster," remembering how he borrowed your Chipmunks album and left it in the sun; and then, when you got mad, he had the audacity to claim the album actually was *his!*

But your smooth-talking brother persists. He says he'll write a note that states he promises to return the Swiss Army knife to you after he returns from summer camp. Recalling the condition of your album after he borrowed it, you demand that he back up his note by letting you keep his sack of marbles as collateral. He includes a clause to that effect in the note. You sign it, your brother signs it, and, just to play it safe, you have Mom sign it too.

You have just executed a deed of trust, secured by real property. You are the beneficiary (creditor) of the note. Your brother is the trustor (borrower), and your mother is trustee.

The terms "mortgage" and "deed of trust" are used interchangeably, although they are not the same thing. The difference between the two lies in how a foreclosure is executed if the borrower defaults. The use of a mortgage or deed of trust varies from state to state. In California, trust deeds are used almost exclusively. A deed of trust involves the three parties outlined above. The deed of trust, executed by the creditor to secure an obligation (usually a promissory note), is a recorded lien on the property. Only if the borrower defaults on the promissory note does the trustee become involved. The trustee may be any "legal person" (as opposed to an "illegal person"?), although it typically is the title company used to insure the title. In the event you default on the loan, the trustee may sell the property at a "trustee's sale" and apply the proceeds of the sale to satisfy the debt. Promise you'll never learn about foreclosure proceedings first hand.

Should you one day own the property free and clear, there will be no more deeds of trust recorded on the property, only a deed in your name.

"Closing" is the final phase of a home purchase. Final papers are signed and recorded, and money changes hands, all done through escrow. The costs that the seller and buyer incur at this time are called "closing costs." Closing costs include appraisal fee, realtor's commission, lender's charges, advance mortgage payment, hazard insurance payment, mortgage insurance, real estate taxes, and title and escrow fees. Local custom determines who, seller or buyer, pays for which costs.

Since you, the buyer, must typically pay the lender's charges (which could amount to thousands of dollars), you may ease the sting by taking advantage of a quirk in the tax laws. If you pay the loan fee by check, rather than allowing the lender to subtract it from the loan proceeds, the loan fee is fully tax deductible in the year of the sale. If the lender pays the loan fee by withholding it from the loan proceeds, the loan fee must be amortized over the life of the loan.

The escrow period is the time from the seller's acceptance of an offer to the closing, when title is officially transferred to the buyer. During this period, the seller cannot accept any other offers. You may sweeten your offer by stipulating a fast escrow, like 40 days. To assure the seller that you can close this quickly, you should have a "prequalification letter" from a lender, a copy of a clean credit report, and a personal financial statement filled out in detail.

For a discussion of closing and closing costs, get a copy of "Buying a Home? Don't Forget Those Closing Costs!," a free booklet available from lenders or from reference 31. A second free publication, "Understanding Closing and Title Costs," is available from reference 103.

PART THREE

CREATIVE HOME BUYING

In Part One of this book, you solved an equation that determined the house price you could afford. What did you find? Were the results exciting or depressing? The following section is for those people who found they could barely afford to buy a closet. You *can* purchase a home even when conventional wisdom says you can't. The solution is simple: Use unconventional wisdom.

Conventional wisdom dictates that you put 20% down and take out a 30-year, fixed-rate mortgage from the local bank to cover the rest. This method was the mainstay of the housing industry for nearly half a century. It was safe, easy, and predictable. Then came 1980.

With interest rates soaring to 16% in 1980, only one of every six California families could qualify to purchase a median-priced home; the housing industry plummeted into the worst recession since the Great Depression. The beleaguered industry was kept afloat primarily because home buyers took matters into their own hands and began employing "creative financing" techniques to purchase their homes. The banking industry then followed suit by introducing their own forms of creative financing. As will be seen, most of the new methods are either more complicated or more risky for the buyer than the simple 30-year, fixed-rate mortgages. However, these unconventional methods of financing have put home buying within the grasp of millions of families who otherwise would be excluded by excessive home prices and interest rates.

Let's first investigate the creative financing techniques employed by the banking industry. Since a third of all new mortgages are of this type, these techniques, thought to be avant garde in 1980, have now become mainstream.

BANKER'S CREATIVE HOME BUYING

Adjustable Rate Mortgages

When the interest-rate crisis occurred during the early 1980s, financial institutions created a way to make a home loan more affordable. The banks began to tie the interest on a home loan to a variable index, like U.S. treasury bills. Onto this index the institutions tack a "margin" of 1 or 2%, and that determines the interest rate the borrower pays. The interest charged to the borrower is periodically (every year, for example) adjusted by the lender to equal the index plus the margin. Because these loans are less risky for the lender (and more risky for the borrower), the initial interest rate on an "adjustable-rate mortgage" (ARM) is typically 2% lower than the interest rate on a fixed-rate mortgage. Two percent may sound inconsequential. However, by plugging a 2% lower interest rate into the equation in Figure 3, you discover a radical difference in the house price you can afford.

Adjustable-rate mortgages are composed of a baffling array of variables. And, just to guarantee total confusion, each bank adds its own peculiarities to these variables. Locating the "best" ARM requires either an MBA or a systematic approach. Let's try a systematic approach. Figure 14 lists three different ARMs. First we'll examine the various parameters that make up an ARM, and then compare the three ARMs to determine which is best. Like fixed-rate loans, these loans are typically fully amortized 30-year loans. As stated earlier, the institution tacks a margin of 1 or 2% onto the index, and the total is the interest rate the borrower is charged. At the end of each adjustment period, the lender adjusts the interest rate charged to reflect any changes in the index.

Figure 14. Adjustable Rate Mortgage Table

Parameter	Bank A	Bank B	Bank C
Init. int. rate	10.4%	8.95%	9.25%
Points	2%	2%	1.5%
Index	6 Mo. TB	11 COF	11 COF
Margin	2.75%	2.875%	2.625%
Index + margin	11.35%	11.22%	10.975%
Life cap	6%	14.75%	15.25%
Adjustment cap	1%	1%	none *
Adjustment per.	6 months	6 months	1 year
Negative amort.	no	no	yes

*Payment adjustment cap of 7.5%

Since the interest rate is determined by the index and margin, these two parameters should be given the most consideration in choosing an adjustable mortgage. Comparing margins is straightforward--the smaller the better. Comparing indexes, on the other hand, requires a bit more thought.

The three most popular indexes are the six-month Treasury bill, the one-year Treasury security, and the regional Cost of Funds. The best index, from the borrower's perspective, is the one with the lowest average rate over the life of the loan. This of course requires predicting the future economy--a somewhat difficult task. However, the next best thing to predicting the future is learning from the past. Therefore, let's investigate the past performance of these indexes and decree the index that has historically been the lowest as the "best" index.

Gushing about its relative stability, the sweetheart of both banks and real estate experts is the Cost of Funds index. However, after a casual glance at Figure 15, this romance with the Cost of Funds index seems questionable (at least coming from anyone on the side of consumers).

Assume that in 1981 you had a choice between two loans, exactly alike except that one was tied to the six-month Treasury bill and the other was tied to the Cost of Funds. Had you ignored the advice of real estate experts and taken the loan tied to the six-month T-bill, nine years later you would have paid an average of .9% lower interest. And had you made the same choice in 1985, the results are even more dramatic: Four years later you would have paid an average of 1.3% less interest on the loan indexed to the six-month T-bill compared to the same loan indexed to the Cost of Funds. On a $150,000 loan, this amounts to a savings of about $10,000 over five years. Contrary to popular wisdom, of the most common indexes, the six-month T-bill is the best, with the Cost of Funds and one-year Treasury security tied for second place.

Another feature of ARMs is the initial interest rate discount. The discount can be seen in Figure 14 by comparing the initial interest rate to the index plus margin. Whenever there is an initial interest-rate discount, the interest charged the borrower will change at each adjustment until the interest charged equals the index plus the margin. Therefore, even if the index doesn't change, the interest rate will increase. Too often borrowers choose a loan based entirely upon the initial interest rate. While it is nice to have an initial interest rate discount, the impact of the discount is fleeting. The honeymoon ends after the first or second adjustment. On the other hand, other features, like the margin and adjustment cap, impact your payments for as long as you hold the loan.

Figure 15. Index History Graph

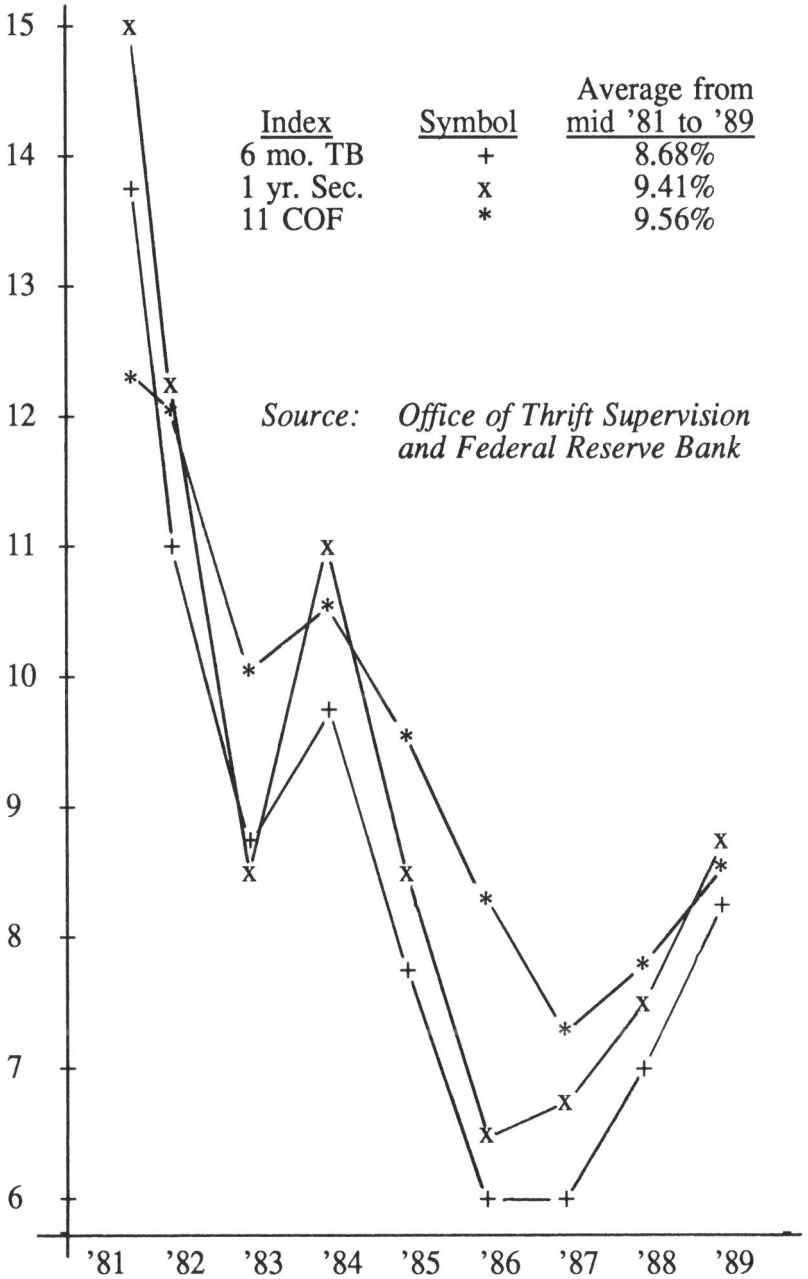

Index	Symbol	Average from mid '81 to '89
6 mo. TB	+	8.68%
1 yr. Sec.	x	9.41%
11 COF	*	9.56%

Source: *Office of Thrift Supervision and Federal Reserve Bank*

To make these adjustable loans more appealing to borrowers, banks have built certain safeguards into the loans. One safeguard is a limit ("cap") on the amount the interest may change over the life of the loan. The consumer is further protected by an adjustment cap, which limits the amount the interest may adjust at one time.

So which of the three adjustable loans in Figure 14 is best? Let's first compare Bank A to Bank B. Recalling that the index and margin should be given the most weight in comparing loans, we immediately lean toward Bank A, since its margin is lower than Bank B and its index is the preferred six-month T-bill. If its other features are okay, Bank A wins. Both lenders charge a 2% loan initiation fee (i.e., 2 points). This loan initiation fee is a one-time fee, charged for the privilege of becoming indentured to the bank for the rest of your life. Both banks re-adjust the interest to equal the index plus the margin every six months, with an allowed maximum adjustment of 1%. Bank A is still winning.

Next compare the lifetime adjustment caps of the two banks. Unfortunately, the two banks specify their interest rate ceilings in two different ways. Bank B states that the interest you are charged will never exceed 14.75%. Bank A states that the amount the interest may change over the life of the loan will never exceed 6%. Therefore the maximum interest Bank A charges is 10.4% + 6% = 16.4%. But let's call Bank A just to be sure. Upon doing so, we find that, yes, the lifetime rate adjustment cap is 6%, but that cap is based on the initial index plus the margin (11.35%), not on the initial interest rate you are required to pay (10.4%). So now the overall lifetime cap from Bank A is 11.35% + 6% = 17.35%. To avoid this confusion, always request the absolute lifetime interest cap, as listed by Bank B. Bank B's lifetime adjustment cap is lower, and therefore better for the borrower. Bank B has gained slightly on Bank A.

The initial interest rate of Bank B is lower by 1.4%. But, as shown in Figure 16, that gap is closed after just two adjustment periods. The easiest way to compare different interest-rate discounts is to view them in the same way you view loan initiation fees, as temporary costs. So over the first year, the loan from Bank A costs about 1.4% more than the loan from Bank B. Bank A could have essentially achieved the same thing by offering the same initial interest discount as Bank B, but charged an extra 1.4 points. Bank B has gained even more on Bank A.

Figure 16 How the Loans in Figure 14 Vary Over Two Years
(Assuming their indexes don't change)

	Bank A	Bank B	Bank C
Initial	10.4	8.95	9.25
6 months	11.35	8.95	9.25
1 year	11.35	10.95	10.975[1]
1.5 years	11.35	11.225	10.975
2 years	11.35	11.225	10.975[2]

Notes:
1. The payment adjustment cap limits the payment adjustment to about 10.1%.
2. At this change period, the payment adjusts to match the interest charged.

Having compared all the important parameters, which loan is best? Bank B has a better lifetime cap. So lean toward Bank B if you are pessimistic about the economy and you feel we could have the same interest-rate crisis we had in the early '80s. Also, that initial interest-rate discount from Bank B is nice. But the effect of the lower initial interest decreases the longer you own the home. If you plan to live in the home just two or three years, Bank B wins. But, if you're an optimist and you plan to stay in the house for more than five years, the loan from Bank A is preferable.

Let's next compare Bank A to Bank C. In reviewing Bank C we come upon a new term: "negative amortization." Recall that "amortization" means that the remaining loan balance decreases with each payment. Negative amortization means that the amount of money owed the bank may actually increase over the life of the loan. This is because the interest rate of the "note" may be higher than the interest rate you pay.

For example, let's say you borrow $100 from a friend for one year. The interest rate she charges you is 24%, interest only. So over the course of the year she will charge you $24, payable in monthly installments of $2. However, since she's a nice person, she says that during the year you need only pay her at 12% interest or $1 per month. So the interest you are charged is 24%, yet over the one-year life of the loan you are only required to reimburse her at a rate of 12%. She adds the difference between the amount you are charged and the amount you actually pay to your loan balance. Therefore, at the end of the year, you owe her $112, or $12 more than you initially borrowed! This is negative amortization.

Most people shy away from negative amortization. However, I view it simply as "borrowing" a little more money each month to assist in making the monthly payment. This borrowed money is then added to the overall sum owed. There are two conditions under which negative amortization should be avoided. First, when the house is not appreciating in value at a rate that keeps pace with the potentially increasing loan balance, and second, when the initial down payment is less than 20%.

Returning to Figure 14, notice that there is no adjustment cap on Bank C's note. However, the footnote states that Bank C has a payment adjustment cap of 7.5%. What gives? The adjustment cap of 7.5% is a cap on the interest you *pay*. But there is no limit on the change in interest of the note, except for the 15.25% lifetime cap. For example, at the first adjustment of Bank C's loan, the interest rate you are charged jumps immediately to equal the index plus the margin, 10.975%. This would change your loan payment by about 16%. However, the amount your monthly loan payment may change is limited to 7.5%. The difference between what you are charged and what you pay is added to your loan balance, resulting in negative amortization.

To compare a loan with negative amortization to a loan without it, compare the interest you are *charged*, not the interest you are required to *pay*. If the notes seem comparable (i.e., the amounts charged seem comparable), you may prefer the one with negative amortization because the payments may be lower.

In this case, we again begin by comparing the most important parameters, the index and the margin. Bank C has a lower margin, but is indexed to the less desirable Cost of Funds. Recall that the lifetime adjustment cap of Bank A is 17.35%. Therefore, the lifetime interest rate limit of Bank C is better. The loan initiation fee of Bank C is lower by half a point. Furthermore, as can be determined from Figure 16, the average interest of Bank C is lower than Bank A by about 1.5% during the first year of the loan. (After the first year, the two loans charge nearly the same interest, about 11%.) The total initial cost of Bank C's loan is therefore about 2% lower than Bank A's. Just as reasoned earlier, if you plan to live in the home just a few years, Bank C's loan is the one for you. But if you plan to remain in the home more than three years Bank A's loan is best.

Although adjustable-rate mortgages may initially seem about as logical as the electoral college, the concepts eventually make sense. As an aid to comparing ARMS, Bay Area newspapers publish rate tables similar to the one in Figure 14. (Bay Area mortgage tables will be discussed further.)

If you can qualify for an adjustable-rate mortgage and a fixed-rate mortgage, which should you take? The theoretical answer to this question is simple. If, while you hold the loan, the interest rate on the adjustable loan averages lower than the interest rate of the fixed loan, the adjustable is better. However, it's impossible to predict future fluctuations in interest rates. Therefore, although the above theory is perfectly correct, it is also perfectly useless. A rule of thumb is: When interest rates are high (as in 1981), an adjustable mortgage is best. When interest rates are low (as they are now), a fixed-rate mortgage is a better idea. Keep in mind that conventional fixed-rate mortgages are not assumable but adjustables usually are. Therefore, if you plan to sell in the near future, an adjustable-rate mortgage is best. Perhaps the most popular reason for obtaining an adjustable-rate mortgage is that it's easier to qualify for, because typically the lender qualifies you based on the discounted rate, which is about 2% lower than a fixed rate. But, as stated earlier, this bargain rate ends after one or two adjustments. For example, when Figure 14 was created, the average interest on fixed-rate mortgages was 11%. Within one year all three adjustable loans are about 11%, as shown in Figure 16. For further information, order the "Handbook on Adjustable-Rate Mortgages" from reference 8 or "Consumer Guide to Adjustable-Rate Mortgages" from reference 93.

Although an adjustable-rate mortgage is riskier for the consumer, it is a straightforward way to qualify for a larger loan, thus eliminating an enormous barrier to home ownership for many people.

Private Mortgage Insurance

Another barrier faced by today's home buyer is the 20% down payment required by lenders. For a median-priced home in the Bay Area, this amounts to over $50,000--a rather ominous figure. But homes are sold daily with less than 20% down. In fact, over half of today's home buyers put down less than 20%. With a basic understanding of how lending institutions do business, you will see where the 20% figure originated and how to avoid it.

Most lenders don't retain the loans they originate in their portfolios. Usually loans are sold on the "secondary" market to investors. The lender continues to service the loan by sending statements and collecting payments. However, the payments are sent by the initiating lender to the investor who bought the loan. For this service the lender receives an annual fee from the investor.

The two largest buyers of home loans are the Federal National Mortgage Association and the Federal Home Loan Mortgage Corporation, known in cutesy banker talk as Fannie Mae and Freddie Mac, respectively. These corporations are federally chartered but privately owned. Both companies buy only loans that fall within their strict guidelines. As a result, many lenders structure their loan packages to meet the criteria of Fannie Mae or Freddie Mac. FNMA and FHLMC have decreed they *will* buy loans that exceed 80% of the purchase price. However, they stipulate that in such cases the buyer must obtain "private mortgage insurance" (PMI). This PMI insures the lender against possible losses should the homeowner default on the mortgage. Private mortgage insurance costs home buyers an additional .25 to .4% over their regular interest rate. If PMI is required, the lender will request that the insurance premium be included every month with the regular principal and interest payment. The loan papers should specify that PMI will no longer be required once the loan balance falls below 80% of the home value (either due to appreciation or due to a decreased loan balance).

Incidentally, Fannie Mae has a maximum gross income to PITI (principal, interest, taxes, and insurance) ratio of 28%. That is why, in Part One, 28% was used in determining what a buyer could afford. To reduce the number of foreclosures on houses carrying low down payments, Fannie Mae requires that the PITI payments be less than 25% of your gross monthly income (as opposed to 28%) when the down payment is between 5% and 10% (5% is FNMA's minimum).

A question often asked regarding the down payment is, "Shouldn't I put down as much as possible, so I don't have to pay so much interest to a bank?" There are pros and cons to a large down payment. Here are a few points to consider.

In favor of a large down payment:
1. When the interest rate on the loan is greater than the interest rate you are earning on your money, a large down payment is indicated. For example, if you are

collecting 7% interest on your investments, then that is the cost of investing that money in a down payment. If the bank is charging 9% on the loan, then that is the cost of not investing that money in a down payment, and instead borrowing more from the bank. So, in this example, the cost of investing in a down payment is less than the cost of borrowing from the bank.

2. A larger down payment may allow you to avoid PMI premium payments. On a $200,000 loan, PMI could cost $800 annually. However, not all lenders sell to Fannie Mae and Freddie Mac, and therefore may allow a down payment as low as 10% without requiring PMI.

In favor of a low down payment:

1. A large loan that can be assumed by a subsequent buyer helps tremendously when you sell.

2. The peace of mind afforded by a safety net in your bank account for emergencies or other investments suggests a low down payment.

3. When the interest the lender is charging is less than the interest you are making on your money, a low down payment is indicated.

Fifteen-Year Mortgages

To make monthly loan payments affordable, recall that lenders amortize fixed-rate loans over 30 years. However, lenders have discovered that some home buyers qualify for loans amortized over fewer years. Because the loan must be repaid over fewer years, the monthly loan payments are higher on a 15-year loan than on a 30-year loan. However, since there are fewer years of interest payments, the overall interest paid to the lender is less. So, for those home buyers who can qualify for the larger monthly payments, a reduced mortgage life represents thousands of dollars in savings.

Most lenders offer 15-year mortgages. These mortgages are not "creative" in the strict sense, because they are more difficult, not less difficult, to qualify for. But if you can qualify for the loan amount you need, a 15-year mortgage renders some savings over the long term.

Figure 17. Comparison of a 15- and a 30-Year Fully Amortized $100,000 Mortgage After 15 Years

	30-Year	15-Year
Interest rate	10%	9.5%
Monthly payments	$ 878	$ 1,044
Gross monthly income required to qualify	3,200	3,800
Loan balance after:		
5 years	96,574	80,606
10 years	90,938	49,407
15 years	81,665	0
Total interest payments after 15 years	139,705	87,920
15-year summary:		
Loan balance	81,665	0
Money paid[1]	158,040	187,920
Tax savings[2]	-39,117	-24,618
Interest income[3]	-23,406	-0
Net money paid plus remaining liability:	$ 177,182	$ 163,302

Notes:
1. Total paid = (Monthly payments) x 12 x 15
2. Tax savings = (Interest payments) x .28
3. After tax interest income on $1,992/year.

As an example, let's examine a 15-year and a 30-year fixed-rate mortgage of $100,000. We will compare the two loans after 15 years of mortgage payments. The interest on a 15-year mortgage is typically 1/2% lower than a 30-year mortgage. As shown in Figure 17, the 30-year mortgage carries an interest rate of 10%, while the interest rate on the 15-year mortgage is 9.5%. Note that the gross monthly income required to qualify for the 15-year mortgage is indeed greater than for the 30-year mortgage. To make the comparison fair, assume that the self-disciplined 30-year borrower invests the money saved by the lower mortgage payments. This amounts to $1,992 annually and earns an after-tax interest rate of 6.5%.

After the 15-year mark, the 15-year borrower has paid about $30,000 more than the 30-year borrower. However, the 30-year borrower still owes the bank almost $82,000. The 15-year borrower, on the other hand, owes nothing. The loan is completely paid off. All things considered, the 15-year borrower fairs better than the 30-year borrower by about $14,000, saving approximately $1,000 per year over the 15-year period.

Note that the net cost of the 30-year mortgage would be much greater if the 30-year borrower did not make the annual deposits of $1,992 over the years. In this respect, a 15-year mortgage may be considered a forced savings account. Many prominent banks and real estate journalists have touted 15-year mortgages as rendering savings of as much as $100,000. These new mortgages do provide some savings, but not nearly as much as consumers have been led to believe. For further details, request "How a 15-Year Mortgage Can Help You Save for the Future" from reference 93.

Prepaying Principal

Instead of obtaining a 15-year mortgage, you may achieve the same result by prepaying some of the principal. To prepay the principal you simply include extra money with your monthly mortgage payment. That money is then used by the bank to reduce your loan balance. The advantage of prepaying principal on a 30-year mortgage over obtaining a 15-year mortgage is that you control when you make the extra payments--the extra payments are not dictated by the loan agreement. Referring to Figure 17, in the early years of the loan you may feel more comfortable with the $878 monthly loan payments of the 30-year loan. Later, as your income increases, you may begin to add extra principal payments to your mortgage payments. The disadvantage of this method is that you do not get the benefit of the half-percent interest discount carried by the 15-year mortgage. The impact of prepaying principal is different between adjustable and fixed-rate loans. In both cases you reduce the principal balance. The effect of a reduced balance on a fixed-rate loan is to reduce the life of the loan, from 30-years to 20-years, for example. But your monthly loan payments remain the same. To realize the benefit of having invested your extra hard-earned money in the loan, you must either sell the house or live in it until the loan is paid off in 20 instead of 30 years. In contrast, the life of an adjustable loan is not reduced when extra principal payments are made; it remains at 30 years. Instead, you discover the happy consequence of having made the extra principal payments the next time the loan adjusts. Since the lender determines your new loan payments based upon your reduced loan balance, your loan payments are reduced. It is as if you had invested the extra principal payments at an interest rate equal to the interest rate of the loan. It can be shown (with cumbersome mathematics) that over the life of the loan, the total amount paid to the bank is the same whether you prepay a fixed or adjustable loan. But when prepaying an adjustable you are rewarded almost immediately with lower loan payments.

Mortgage Shopping

A house is probably not the most expensive item you'll ever purchase. The most expensive item you'll ever purchase is a mortgage. Over its life, a loan costs two or three times the price tag of a house. Hunt for financing with the same care and consideration you give your housing search.

An average-priced home may be magically transformed into a bargain with the right financing package. Unfortunately, lenders offering cut-rate financing aren't grouped together in the phone book. Furthermore, a bargain basement one week may be Gump's the next. Locating factory-outlet financing is not a question of where you look, but rather of how you look.

The pain of mortgage shopping has been eased in the past few years by the proliferation of mortgage-rate surveys. These surveys outline the loan origination fees and interest rates of many lenders. For adjustable-rate mortgages, these tables also specify the features indicated in Figure 14. Many local papers print mortgage tables every week, as shown in Figure 11. Mortgage surveys are also available from references 94 through 98.

The primary problem with mortgage surveys is that most lenders do not guarantee (or "lock in") their interest rate upon receipt of the loan application. Typically, the interest rate is locked in when the loan is approved, which may be four to eight weeks after the application is submitted. So a lender may lower its rate, receive a flood of applications, and then raise its rate again before it approves any loans.

Figure 18. Questions to Ask About Mortgages

Questions relevant to both fixed and adjustable mortgages:
1. What is the interest rate?
2. What is the loan initiation fee?
3. Is the loan assumable at the original terms?
      How many times may it be assumed and what is the assumption fee?
4. What is the prepayment penalty?
5. Is PMI required?
      Once the loan balance falls below 80% of the house value, is PMI waived?
6. Is the rate locked in upon application?
      When does the rate guarantee period expire?
      What if the period expires as the result of the lender's delays?
7. What are the estimated closing costs?
8. Once the loan application paper work is all in, how many days before the loan is approved? (It should be less than a week.)
9. References from three recent borrowers?

Questions relevant only to adjustable mortgages:
10. Can the loan be converted to a fixed-rate mortgage?
      Is there a conversion fee or other restrictions?
      In order to be attractive, the conversion fee
      should be substantially less than the cost to
      execute a new loan.
11. Is negative amortization possible?
12. What is the initial interest rate?
      Is there an initial interest discount?
      What is the current index plus margin?
      How might the interest rate change once the
      discount period expires?
13. What is the lifetime cap on the interest rate?
14. What is the adjustment cap?
15. What is the index?
      What is the adjustment period? Ask the lender
      to show you a chart depicting the five-year
      history of the index.
16. What margin is added to the index to determine the
    interest rate?
17. Is there a carry-over provision allowing the lender to
    counter the adjustment cap?
      If the interest rises more than the cap allows,
      these sneaky provisions allow the lender to
      carry over the extra unpaid interest and tack it
      onto next year's bills.

The lender should show you the answers to these questions in the loan documents.

You may protect yourself from this abusive treatment
in three ways. First, always ask if the terms of the loan
are locked in upon receipt of the application, and ask
when the lock-in period expires. If the loan terms are
guaranteed upon application, be sure to get that
agreement in writing. The lender may increase the interest rate or charge extra points in exchange for this lock-
in provision, which in turn decreases the value of the

guarantee. A guaranteed rate is less crucial when interest
rates are stable or declining.

A second defense against lenders' whims is to apply
to lenders with consistently low rates. If a lender's rate is
low week after week, a lock-in provision becomes less
important. Determine which lenders are consistently low
by monitoring a number of mortgage surveys for a few
weeks.

To reduce the chance of becoming another notch in a
banker's mahogany desk, apply to three lenders. This
third technique will cost you more in the short term
(nonrefundable application fees are about $200 to $300),
but may save you thousands of dollars in the long term.
In this way, you will not be victimized by a bank that
processes your loan with the same urgency that the IRS
returns your tax refund. Nor will you be left without
alternatives should the lender increase the interest rate at
the last moment.

The difficulty of comparing adjustable-rate mortgages
is supposedly reduced by the Truth-in-Lending Act,
which requires lenders to inform borrowers of the
"annual percentage rate" (APR). In addition to the simple
interest rate, the APR takes into account all initiation fees
paid to the lender. As such, APRs should provide a more
accurate representation of the true interest rate. Unfortunately, two lenders may offer the exact same loan
package yet arrive at APR figures that differ dramatically. Therefore, the APR is unfortunately a meaningless
tool for comparing adjustable-rate loans of different
lenders.

One final note on mortgage shopping. In general,
fixed-rate loans that carry bargain interest rates have
higher loan initiation fees. But over time the higher
initial fee is compensated for by the lower rate. For
example, Loan A carries an interest rate .5% lower than
Loan B. But Loan A's loan initiation fee is 1.5 points
higher than Loan B. If you anticipate remaining in the
house more than three years, Loan A is the better choice.

As a guide to mortgage shopping, Figure 18 offers a
list of questions to ask the lender about any given loan.

PEOPLE'S CREATIVE HOME BUYING

All the preceding methods of reducing the cost of home purchase--obtaining an adjustable mortgage, insuring a low down payment with PMI, obtaining a 15-year mortgage, and careful comparison shopping--have become well-established practices. However, none of these methods may be sufficient if: (1) you can't afford a conventional home, (2) you don't have enough money for a down payment or (3) you don't have enough income to qualify for an institutional loan. These cases call for more radical purchase techniques. In fact, even if you can qualify for an institutional loan on a conventional home, creative home buying may yield a better deal.

Bargain Homes

The risk in buying a cheap home is that it may be even *cheaper* by the time you decide to sell. This is known, in sophisticated real estate jargon, as "a lousy deal." However, by observing certain precautions, you can minimize the inherent risk in buying an inexpensive home. We shall examine five sources of cheap homes: condominiums, foreclosures, fixer-uppers, new homes, and premarket homes.

Condominiums

The perils of purchasing a condominium are exemplified by the unfortunate experience of a friend of mine. Nancy found an ideal condo for herself--great financing, low down payment, beautiful design, swimming pool, jacuzzi, sauna, and close to her work.

As she was moving in, a neighbor came over to greet her. "You aren't actually moving in, are you?" questioned the neighbor. "Do you know what's going on here?"

Nancy then listened as the neighbor elaborated on one horror story after another. The builder had run into financial troubles. A third of the condominium complex would remain unfinished for an indefinite period of time. Of the two-thirds that was complete, the builder was renting the vacant units, instead of selling them (property values tend to plummet if over 20% of the units are rented). Nancy asked if the lender might bail the builder out of this fix. No, because the finance company itself had just filed bankruptcy!

Nancy spoke to other members of the condominium. One resident after another told stories of inadequate sound insulation, noise from airplanes (the complex was built in the flight path of the local airport), swimming pools never completed, inadequate hot water (the water heaters were sometimes 100 feet from the units they serviced), poor mail service (the developer hadn't supplied mail boxes), and a long fight with the developer just to get lawn furniture for one of the outdoor common areas. When she asked one resident what he was going to do, the answer was simple: "Move as soon as possible."

You can avoid Nancy's dilemma by doing a little research prior to purchasing a condominium. The primary complaint of condominium owners is poor construction, especially inadequate sound proofing between adjoining condos. To check the building's insulation, ask neighbors above, below, and to the sides to turn on a TV or stereo and listen from inside your unit. Also, ask the condo owners' association about any other structural problems. The owners' association can also provide you with its latest financial statement. Unless a portion of the monthly maintenance fee is set aside to cover emergencies, expect a large special assessment when a major repair becomes necessary. Because nonresident owners want to keep monthly fees at a minimum, maintenance quality decreases in direct proportion to the number of rented units. Carefully examine how well both the building and common area are maintained. In a new building, determine how many of the units have sold. As many frustrated Bay Area condo owners will testify, never be among the first buyers in a new complex. For every unit the developer still owns, the developer has one vote in the condo owners' association. Believe me, you do not want a developer who is losing money as a general partner in building maintenance and management. Furthermore, you do not want to compete with unsold new units when you decide to sell your condo.

Condominiums appreciate slower than single-family homes. Between 1982 and 1988, the average appreciation of condominiums in California was 2% annually (compared to a statewide annual appreciation rate of 7% on single-family homes over the same period). Nevertheless, condominiums make excellent starter homes. Just be sure to thoroughly investigate the complex before you buy. See reference 148 for further information.

Foreclosed Homes

In addition to condominiums, foreclosed homes also provide an opportunity to purchase an inexpensive house. Recall that all lenders hold the property as collateral via a deed of trust. In the event a borrower fails to make the mortgage payments, the lender can repossess the property.

There are three time periods during which distressed property may become available for purchase. The first time is after the Notice of Default has been filed against the borrower. Following the Notice of Default, the borrower has three months (in California) to reinstate the mortgage. To do this, the borrower must make up any missed loan payments and pay any trustee fees and expenses. During this period, the borrower may very well wish to sell the property, often at a discount.

To find borrowers in this unfortunate quandary, contact the county clerk who records notices of mortgage default. In urban areas, this information may be obtained by subscribing to a local public recording summary service. The county clerk or a title insurance firm can tell you if such a service exists in your area. Reference 19 provides a listing of various foreclosure summary services.

The second opportunity to purchase foreclosed property is at the foreclosure sale. These sales require the buyer to put up full cash payment, and therefore are of little interest to first-time home buyers.

The final opportunity to purchase foreclosed property is after the foreclosure sale. If there are no bidders at the foreclosure sale, the lender takes title to the property.

The repossessed property that the lender holds is called REO (real estate owned). Most lenders are anxious to get rid of these properties, and sell them at very favorable terms. Contact each lender's REO officer. Ask if the lender presently holds any REOs, and request that you be notified as new properties become available. Also request the name and phone number of the realty firm that handles the lender's REO portfolio.

The U.S. Housing and Urban Development Department publishes its repossessed homes weekly in the classified section of the Sunday *Examiner*. The newspaper announcement also explains how to bid on these houses. Call the VA at the beginning of the month for a list of its repossessed homes. For information on Fannie Mae foreclosures, see reference 93. Furthermore, all the agencies in the reference section that provide government-sponsored loans also hold repossessed homes.

Fixer Uppers

You may find that homes you can afford are not in mint condition. So even if you don't harbor the romantic desire to transform your living environment into a unique reflection of your personality, you may find yourself with a paintbrush in one hand and a hammer in the other.

Luckily, a house requiring repairs typically is cheaper than a comparable home in perfect condition. But if the cost to rehabilitate the home is greater than the discount on the home, you aren't getting a bargain. Nevertheless, bargains are out there if you know what to look for.

The work a house requires falls into one of two categories: repair or remodel work. Many homes need both types of rehabilitation. Usually repair work is hidden to the casual observer but remodel work isn't. Repair work includes, for example, restoring the foundation, renovating the electrical system, or replacing the water heater. Remodel work may involve replacing the kitchen cabinets, adding a bathroom, painting the exterior, or refinishing the floors.

The first rule-of-thumb is: Repair work loses money, remodel work doesn't. To prove this rule to yourself, simply listen to your spouse or partner as he or she expounds on the virtues of homes you have seen. How often do you hear "Oh darling, let's buy the one with that cute new foundation"? Furthermore, you quickly discover that homes requiring $30,000 of repair work are only $15,000 less than the going rate in the neighborhood. On the other hand, a house needing only a $1,000 face lift may be $10,000 below market value. The reason for this is simple: out of sight, out of mind. Potential purchasers are more concerned with the paint peeling off the walls than with the termites chewing on the floor joists.

The second rule-of-thumb is: Turn repairing into remodeling to add value. For example, while replacing the old roof, spend a little extra and add a couple of sky lights. Now you have transformed a repair, which is a money drain, into a remodel, which enhances the value of the home.

The third rule-of-thumb is: Remodeling jobs are not all created equal. You can not recoup the cost of all remodeling jobs upon selling. According to statistics culled from various organizations in the remodeling industry, the top three jobs rendering the greatest return on investment are (in order of return potential): fireplace addition, bathroom addition, and minor kitchen remodel. The organizations excluded from their studies simpler work, like landscaping or painting the interior. According to real estate professionals, these less expensive jobs probably render an even greater return per dollar.

The fourth rule-of-thumb is: Don't create the most expensive house on the block. As such, it's best to renovate the worst house in the neighborhood to make it comparable with average homes in the area.

If you intend to do the work yourself, I strongly recommend taking a class from the Owner Builder Center (reference 123). Should you decide to have a contractor do the work, contact the Contractors State Licensing Board (reference 120) and the Better Business

Bureau to check past complaints or legal actions taken against the contractor. The remodeling industry ranks in the top ten on the Council of Better Business Bureaus' consumer complaint list. With this in mind, it is prudent to require a formal contract with any contractor. Standardized contracts may be obtained from reference 116.
    One final note. Many local governments provide rehabilitation loans at very favorable terms. Check the reference section for government programs in your area.

New Homes
    At the other end of the spectrum from fixer-uppers are new homes. When the real estate market is booming, most developers will not negotiate on price. However, during slow housing periods, anxious home builders may be an excellent source of bargains. Also, developers offer buyers a discount of a few thousand dollars when purchasing homes from blueprints or when purchasing early in the building cycle. But to guard against your new home quickly degenerating into a fixer-upper, thoroughly investigate the builder prior to purchasing. If homes in the new development have been sold, ask residents if they are satisfied both with the quality of their homes and with the response of the builder to complaints. If homes in the new development have not yet been sold, visit other projects the builder has completed. Using information from the county recorder's office, you may determine the appreciation rate of homes in the builder's previous subdivisions. Also, ask to see a copy of the builder's warranty, and be sure you understand what amenities are (and are not) included. The top ten Bay Area builders are listed in references 106 through 115.

Premarket Purchase
    Condominiums are less expensive because they are cheaper to build and less desirable to own. Foreclosures are less expensive because they are more difficult to buy and unwanted by the sellers. Fixer-uppers are less expensive because they entail a lot of work. But what about houses that are less expensive because they are

simply a good deal? Part Two described some bargain-hunting tricks. Let's explore one source of bargains not touched upon in Part Two: buying a house before it is put on the market. By purchasing before the property is advertised, you've automatically eliminated all your competition and bypassed realty agents and their commissions. Within the limits set by the seller, you can write your own ticket.

To find a house before it is advertised, you must either find someone who is about to sell or someone who can be persuaded to sell. To locate someone thinking of selling a home, your best avenue is good old word of mouth. Let it be known to friends and relatives that you are in the market. Ask your doctor, banker, hair cutter, or dentist if they know of a potential seller. It is, unfortunately, a hit-and-miss method.

However, locating someone who may be *persuaded* to sell a home is not as hit and miss. Landlords are ripe potential sellers, waiting to be harvested. For starters, if you like the house in which you presently live, ask the landlord about buying it. All landlords live in the shadow of monthly mortgage payments just like homeowners. When rental owners receive 30-days' notice from tenants, they may not be able to afford the lost rental income while waiting for the property to sell. Therefore, they simply put the home back on the rental market. However, if you approach them at this time, while they are hassling with new paint jobs and finding new tenants, they may be very willing to wash their hands of the whole mess and sell to you. Rental ads are overflowing with owners in this exact quandary. Call on homes that interest you and ask the landlord if he or she would consider selling.

Furthermore, property owners' associations are comprised of disgruntled landlords bound together by their common hatred of rent control. These associations all have newsletters in which you may place an ad announcing your interest in buying a house. The California Apartment Association (reference 147) can direct you to property owners' associations in your area. Also, by rummaging through the public files at the

Berkeley, Oakland, or San Francisco rent boards, you may determine which rental owners recently faced legal battles with tenants. A landlord who is reeling from a recent court skirmish might love to get rid of the property.

The Low Down

Aside from obtaining PMI, what are other methods of buying a home with a minimal down payment? We will examine three methods of buying with a low down payment: (1) VA and FHA loans, (2) lease with option to buy, and (3) shared equity. This is by no means an exhaustive list of how to purchase property with little cash. The sources listed in the reference section give further details.

FHA and VA Loans

The Federal Housing Administration (which is a subdivision of the U.S. Housing and Urban Development Department) and the Veteran's Administration both provide insurance to the lender in the event you default on your loan. Neither of the agencies actually supply the money, which is obtained through mortgage brokers.

VA loans have some advantages over FHA loans. The VA doesn't require a down payment on the house; it provides 100% financing. FHA loans, on the other hand, require about a 5% down payment. Furthermore, the VA has a higher loan limit, $184,000 as opposed to a $124,875 limit on FHA loans. The charge for the VA loan guarantee is 1% of the total loan, whereas the FHA charges 3.8% for its loan insurance. A disadvantage of VA loans is that they are only available to veterans, although anyone may assume a VA loan.

As mentioned earlier, most fixed-rate mortgages are not assumable by subsequent buyers. However, with certain restrictions, both VA and FHA loans are assumable. A disadvantage of both VA and FHA loans is that you must wait patiently while bureaucratic wheels slowly turn. The sluggish government gears may be greased if the lender has "auto approval" authority from the VA or "direct endorsement" authority from the FHA. Both agencies require the mortgage insurance premium to be paid when the loan is originated, as opposed to paying the premium in monthly installments, as with PMI. This can be a substantial chunk of money. Figure 19 summarizes FHA and VA loans.

Figure 19. FHA and VA Loan Specifications

 FHA
Loan limit for single-family home: $124,875
Down payment:
   3% of the first $25,000, 5% of the loan amount above $25,000.
Loan guarantee fee (paid by borrower to FHA):   3.8%
   This fee is returned to the borrower on a prorated basis upon selling. The fee may be financed, even if the loan then exceeds the $124,875 limit.
Lender's fee (paid by borrower to lender):   1%
Discount points[1]:
   The interest rate is not set by FHA. If a below-market rate is desired, then discount points are negotiated between lender and borrower.
Qualifying ratios[2]:
   Housing expense ratio: <29%
   Long term debt ratio: <41%

 VA
Loan limit for single-family home: $184,000
Down payment: none required
Loan guarantee fee (paid by borrower to VA):   1%
   Fee may be financed, but loan amount can never exceed $184,000.
Lender's fee (paid by borrower to lender):   1%

Discount points[1]:
   The interest rate is set by the VA. To offset the difference between current market rates and VA limits, the lender charges discount points. The seller is required by the VA to pay these points.

Qualifying ratios[2]:

Residual income (two people) :   > $733

Long-term debt ratio: < 41%

Residual income is the income remaining after subtracting the following from an applicant's gross monthly income: PITI, monthly debt obligations, maintenance, utilities, and all federal, state, social security, and SDI taxes. See lender for details.

Long-term debt ratio =

$$\frac{\text{PITI + monthly long-term debt payments}}{\text{gross monthly income}}$$

Notes:

1. Discount points are fees the lender charges to offset a lower (i.e., discount) interest rate.
2. The qualifying guidelines of both the VA and FHA are very elastic. Every rule has an exception. This chart doesn't list all the qualifying considerations. See a lender for the full story.

Lease With Option to Buy

The second method of getting into a house for little up-front cash is the short-term lease with an option to buy. For some "consideration for the option" money (usually between $1,000 to $5,000), the seller gives you the option to purchase the house when the lease expires. An agreed-upon portion of the monthly rent payment is applied toward the purchase price if the option is exercised. The option-consideration money is also applied toward the purchase. Until the option is exercised, the seller remains the legal owner, making the mortgage payments with the aid of your monthly rental payment. You do not receive any of the tax write-off benefits until you actually purchase the house.

Note that the lease-option method doesn't lower the down payment, but it does delay the down payment by a few years. In addition to delaying the down payment, the lease option affords three advantages over other methods of home purchase. First you can test out the house before you decide to purchase. Many home buyers, sitting under a leaking roof, wish they could have had this luxury. Second, the lease option ties up a home for two or three years while you improve your financial standing. Third, you lock in the cost of the home now, so there are no surprises two or three years down the road. The agreement specifies an annual increase in the house price to cover appreciation, but often you can negotiate an appreciation figure lower than the actual appreciation.

Homes are usually not advertised as "lease-option" deals, so you, the buyer, must broach the subject with the seller. Good candidates for lease options are houses that have been on the market for a while and houses that were formally rentals. The supreme advocate of lease options is Bob Bruss. Further information can be found in his book (reference 2) or by ordering report #BR87154 ($3.50) from reference 14.

Shared Equity

The third means of purchasing a house with little cash is to have someone else pay the down payment. A person willing to pay your down payment is either a business man or someone who loves you very, very much. I suggest getting it from the latter. This brings mom and dad to mind. But don't call up mom and say, "Gee, I want to buy a house; can I have $10,000?" Call and say, "I have a shared-equity investment opportunity I would like to discuss with you."

Shared equity creates a symbiotic relationship between someone with a good income but little savings (you) and someone with a lot of savings (mom and dad). It works like this: The names of both you and your parents appear on the title and the mortgage. Your parents pay all or part of the down payment. You and your parents decide how to split the interest in the property (50/50, 60/40, etc.). Your parents are the "investors/co-owners." They do not live in the house. You are the "resident/co-owner." You live in the house. Were it not for the IRS, you would simply pay all the mortgage, property taxes, and insurance. However, in order that your parents be allowed to depreciate their portion of the property rented to you, the mortgage, taxes, and insurance are split between you and your parents. You then pay rent to your parents for their share of the house that you are using. Usually this rent covers your parent's portion of the expenses. The contract states that after three to five years the resident will either refinance the home and buy out the investor (at fair market value) or the home will be sold and the profits divided. Thus the name "shared equity."

So you've gotten into a house with little or no down payment, but what do your parents get from this? First, they can deduct "depreciation" on their share of the house that is rented to you. But more importantly, they share in the profits upon selling or refinancing the home. For $3.50 you can receive report #BR87160 from reference 14, which further details shared equity, as does Anderson's book (reference 75). References 80 through 87 match investors with buyers.

Incidentally, if your parents try to pull the old "but tax reform eliminated tax write offs for investors" trick, reassure them that their tax write-off is of utmost concern to you. Explain that if income on their joint return is below $100,000, they may write off up to $25,000 in expenses, such as interest and depreciation. Not only are they now reassured, but they are also very impressed by your sound business knowledge.

If your parents are moved to actually *give* you the down payment (after all, you did let them live with you for eighteen years), then have the down payment transferred to your account three months prior to applying for a loan. Fannie Mae requires that at least 5% of the house cost be your own money. Fannie Mae defines "your own money" as money that has been in your account at least two months.

Obtaining a Loan When the Banker Says You Can't

The down payment is not the only obstacle you face as a first-time home buyer. You must also meet the bank's demand that the monthly mortgage payments absorb less than 28% of your monthly income. If you find you can't qualify for the amount of financing you need, you have three options: (1) pool your resources with others so that you can qualify, (2) borrow from a lender that employs less restrictive qualifying guidelines, (3) borrow from a lender that has lower interest rates.

One or more of these three options are encompassed by each of the following methods of home purchase: cosigner, shared ownership, nonconforming lenders, friends and relatives, seller finance, loan assumption, FHA/VA, and government bonds. We will examine each of these briefly.

Cosigner

If you discover a loan package that suits your needs but you can't meet the qualifying requirements, you may consider obtaining a cosigner on the loan. The bank applies its qualifying ratios to the combined incomes of the primary borrower and the cosigner, thereby making it easier for you to qualify for the loan. Be aware that the lender typically requires the cosigner to sign the deed of trust also. By signing the loan papers with you, the cosigner acts as an insurance policy on the loan. Should you default, the lender will require the cosigner to continue the loan payments. The cosigner must state on subsequent loan applications that she or he has cosigned a loan and may therefore find it difficult to obtain a loan while cosigned on your loan. Essentially a cosigner becomes part owner of the mortgage, with all its associated obligations, without becoming part owner of the house, with all its associated benefits. This sort of martyrdom again suggests mom and dad.

Shared Ownership

The second method is to pool your resources with other people and share ownership of the house. Popularly known as "mingling," this method differs from the shared-equity method mentioned earlier in that all owners occupy the house. There is no "investor." The rule here is "good contracts make good co-owners." Even shared ownership between friends or relatives should be based on a sound contractual agreement. The issues that must be anticipated and spelled out in writing include how the mortgage and down payment are divided, how utilities and maintenance costs are shared, how each party may use the property, how the profits and tax benefits are to be shared, how sales decisions are to be made, and how to deal with a co-owner who cannot or will not meet his or her obligation to the property.

The contract also specifies how title is to be held. The two most popular arrangements are the "limited partnership" and the "tenancy in common agreement." Reference 61, *The Partnership Book*, includes a sample real-estate partnership agreement. Also, Robert Irwin's book (reference 62) is an excellent guide to mingling. Since there are no standard shared-ownership agreement forms, a real-estate attorney should be consulted in structuring the partnership contract.

Another shared housing avenue is the limited-equity cooperative. Typically, a co-op is created by a nonprofit community group or a group of tenants seeking to purchase their building. Structured to limit the profit members may realize upon selling their shares, limited-equity cooperatives put home ownership within the reach of low-income people. References 63 through 74 provide assistance in the creation of shared living arrangements.

All the remaining sources of home loans to be examined embrace both liberal qualifying guidelines and lower interest rates. Even if you can qualify for a conventional bank loan, the following six financing schemes should be investigated. They might save you thousands of dollars.

Nonconforming Lenders

The Federal National Mortgage Association (Fannie Mae) requires that no more than 28% of a borrower's gross monthly income be dedicated to PITI payments. Many buyers find that this restriction makes it impossible to qualify for enough money to buy a Bay Area home. However, not all lenders sell their loans to Fannie Mae.

Lenders that do not are free to employ qualifying guidelines that are more liberal than Fannie Mae's. The average qualifying ratio in the Bay Area is about 35% and some lenders allow up to 40% of a borrower's gross income to go to PITI payments. This allows you to obtain a much larger loan. Such loans are called "nonconforming" (i.e., they don't conform to Fannie Mae's rules). Suspect that a lender is nonconforming if it offers loan amounts over Fannie Mae's limit (which currently is $187,450, but is periodically increased).

Friends and Relatives

Wouldn't it be fun to send your monthly mortgage payment to friends and relatives instead of some cold, impersonal bank? You can do just that, and create a fantastic deal for all parties in the process. By tapping friends and relatives for financing, you avoid the restrictive qualifying policies of conventional lenders and you bypass the bank's loan initiation fee. Furthermore, you can often agree to a below-market interest rate. And the person lending you money usually earns a higher interest than the bank pays. But all your friends are misers? You may be surprised. A friend who is hesitant to lend you $200 for a vacation may be happy to lend you $20,000 for a house, if the loan is secured by a deed of trust. I financed the entire construction of my home in this manner.

Seller Financing

A more likely source of financing is the seller of the property. Seller financing affords the same benefits as borrowing from friends, but avoids all the nasty situations that can arise when mixing friendship and money. In 1984, seller financing accounted for almost 40% of all new mortgages. The seller-financing trend is exciting for the same reason the for-sale-by-owner trend is exciting. It is people taking control of their own financial dealings by eliminating institutions and middle men. It allows the buyer and seller to write their own terms, not just accept the terms dictated by a bank.

Seller financing is illustrated with this example. Bree wants to buy a house and has $10,000 to apply toward a down payment. Aidan is approaching retirement and has owned his home for 20 years. He wants to sell his urban home and buy a house in the country. His original mortgage, executed in 1969 at 6% interest, has an $8,000 balance remaining.

Bree purchases the house for $200,000. She puts down $10,000. If Bree were to obtain a conventional 30-year, fixed-rate bank loan, she would need an annual salary of $60,000 in order to qualify. Furthermore, she would need to pay a loan initiation fee of nearly $4,000.

Figure 20. Seller Financing Example

Purchase price	$ 200,000
Down payment	10,000
Amount financed by seller	$ 190,000
Purchase price	$ 200,000
Balance of existing loan	8,000
Money to seller*	$ 192,000

*This amount is not fully realized until the $190,000 note is paid off in five years by the buyer.

But Aidan agrees to finance the sale himself. He uses part of the down payment to pay off the $8,000 first deed of trust. He then "carries back" a $190,000 note, secured by a new first deed of trust on the property. He and Bree agree to a 9% interest-only loan, with the balloon payment of $190,000 due in five years. Figure 20 illustrates this transaction. Note that although Bree has a $190,000 "loan" from Aidan, he has not actually handed her any money. For Aidan, it's as if he was paid the full $200,000 and immediately took $190,000 and put it in a five-year term account at 9% interest. For Bree, it's as if she got a $190,000 five-year loan from a bank at 9% interest, and immediately paid the $190,000 to Aidan. In five years, both Bree's income and the value of the house will have increased. She should have no trouble obtaining a new mortgage to pay off the balloon in five years. This is a good deal for both Bree and Aidan.

Loan Assumption

Now assume that Bree initially encounters some resistance from Aidan because he needs more than $2,000 (= $10,000 - $8,000) cash out of the deal to help purchase his home in the country. This is a common occurrence with seller financing. But Bree really wants to purchase Aidan's home and suggests that she assume the first deed of trust. To "assume" a loan means to take over the loan at the original terms and interest rate. In 1985, one of every six property purchases involved the assumption of an existing mortgage. A mortgage initiated in 1974 or earlier carries a fixed interest rate of 8.5% or lower.

If the present loan on the property does not contain a legally enforceable "due-on-sale" clause and the interest rate is favorable, you may want to assume the existing loan. A due-on-sale clause in the mortgage or deed of trust gives the lender the power to demand full payment of the loan if the property changes hands. A loan is "assumable" if the lender does not have that power. Most fixed-rate loans initiated today contain due-on-sale clauses. However, many loans executed before 1980 do not carry this stipulation. Most loans available through home mortgage revenue bonds are assumable. Neither FHA nor VA loans contain due-on-sale clauses. Also, any loan sold to Fannie Mae before November 10, 1980, can be assumed at the original terms and interest rate. If asked, the lender is required to divulge if and when the loan was sold to Fannie Mae.

There are two ways to assume a loan. With both methods the buyer must complete the lender's loan assumption application. The first method involves paying an assumption fee and formally assuming the mortgage. The seller is then released from all obligation to the lender. The second method is to purchase the property "subject to" the existing loan. In this case the buyer does not formally assume the loan, and therefore no assumption fee is charged. The seller remains responsible for the loan in the eyes of the lender. For further information on assumable loans, order report #84124 ($3.50) from reference 14.

FHA and VA
Both the FHA and the VA employ liberal qualifying guidelines on their low-interest loans. These agencies take into consideration much more than gross monthly income in determining the loan amount. As outlined in Figure 19, their qualifying ratios are much higher than conventional lenders. Furthermore, by paying extra loan-origination points, the interest rate may be bought down to below-market rates. For example, by paying an additional 2 points, the lender may reduce the interest rate by 1/2 percent.

Government Mortgage Bonds
Because you are a sensitive, caring person, concerned about the welfare of your fellow human beings, you have always voted in favor of state and local housing bond issues. Now is the time to reap what ye hath sown. City, county, and state agencies are overflowing with housing bond money, and they want to give it to you! Not only do they have money to hand you, but their qualification requirements are more liberal, their interest rates are lower, and they charge fewer points than conventional lenders. These loans are usually earmarked for median to low-income first-time home buyers.
Sometimes these bargain loans are fed into the community via developers who pass the loans on to the consumer. In other cases, the loans are available through conventional lenders for the consumer to use for either new or used home purchase. For example, the state of California has mortgage revenue bond money to provide below-market interest rate loans to first-time home buyers. The fixed-rate interest on these 30-year assumable loans is below 9% and they finance up to 95%

of the purchase. Furthermore, as if this weren't enough to make your calculator overheat, they allow a PITI-to-income ratio of 28% (as opposed to the 25% ratio of conventional lenders). The references list a number of bond revenue sources. To find similar agencies in other areas, look under "Housing and Community Development Department" in the government listing section of the phone book.

Unfortunately, despite all the seller financing, adjustable-rate mortgages, and Fannie Maes, this country is in the throes of a serious crisis in housing. In 1981, former President Reagan's Commission on Housing found that one out of every ten households lives in substandard housing. Families wait an average of two years to be allowed into tenement housing projects. Yet, since 1981, low-income housing assistance has been slashed by nearly 80%. And there are those who cannot even afford to rent a house in a slum. In California alone it is estimated that 250,000 people are homeless.

Luckily, there are organizations struggling with this crisis. The California Right to Housing Campaign advocates the housing needs of low-income people at the state capitol. On a national level, the National Low-Income Housing Coalition is fighting a losing battle with the administration to keep 50 years of housing programs from being gutted. Both these organizations need our support and are listed in the resource section.

Well, are you feeling overwhelmed? Does home purchase seem like such a monumental task that you would rather not think about it? Purchasing a home on a tight budget requires common sense, patience, research, and ingenuity. And you can do it! The reference section that follows lists many channels for acquiring both knowledge and financing. And it only scratches the surface of the total resources available.

APPENDIX I

THE GRAND UNIFICATION THEORY OF REAL ESTATE PROFIT AND LOSS

In this section we get dollar signs in our eyes and attempt to answer the question: "Just how filthy rich can I get off of real estate?" I emphasize that money is not the sole consideration in home ownership. But profit motive plays a role in our desire to own a home. Therefore, we should understand the factors which influence a home's investment potential.

In the following discussion, I shall be using the "M" word: mathematics. If you happen to go *catatonic* when staring at an equation, do not fear. If you are willing to accept the equations on faith, you may easily apply the concepts without understanding the arithmetic.

On December 14, 1900, speaking before the German Physical Society, Max Planck first presented the theory of quantized energy. Later, in 1905, Albert Einstein published his celebrated paper on relativity. Scientists subsequently focused on searching for the Big Picture, a theory that would simultaneously accommodate Max Planck's quantum mechanics and Einstein's relativistic phenomena. Today, hidden in the catacombs of Cambridge University, physicist Stephen Hawking continues to struggle with the unification of quantum physics and relativity.

In 1959, Bill Nickerson published his classic *How I Turned $1000 into One Million Dollars in Real Estate*, which described how to pyramid profits by buying fixer-uppers. Riches through rentals was touted in Dave Glubetich's famous *The Monopoly Game*. Robert Allen created a stir in 1980 with his book *Nothing Down*, which outlined the technique of accumulating wealth using other people's money. Following in the footsteps of Stephen Hawking, it seems only appropriate to ask: "What is the big picture?"

Why bother looking for a generalized theory, be it a physics theory or a real estate theory? Good question. A theory helps you to understand the past and, more importantly, to make predictions about the future. And when you live on a planet hurling through space at 66,000 miles per hour, shielded only by a 20-mile cushion of air, any ability to predict the future makes you feel a little less anxious about your situation.

We will develop the big real estate picture by first stating simple facts about the real estate world. We shall then express these facts in a logical mathematical expression. Armed with this equation, we will invade the financial citadels of real estate and leave in our wake a new and deeper understanding of profit and loss.

Let's define profit as the difference between the total money spent on the home during ownership and the total money received upon selling. Notice that this is different from the IRS definition of profit, which defines profit as the difference between the purchase price and the selling price. Our definition, which includes expenditures while owning the home, gives a more realistic financial picture.

Figure 21.
The Grand Unification Theory
of Real Estate Profit and Loss

Simplifying assumptions:
1. Ignore non-mortgage expenses, such as home maintenance, closing costs, property tax, and property insurance.
2. Ignore rent savings (and rent earnings if it is an investment property).
3. Ignore the time value of money.
4. Assume the property is owned less than eight years.

Legend:
P = Purchase price
I_m = After-tax interest rate on loan
I_i = After-tax interest rate on current investment
A = Annual appreciation rate
D = Down payment
N = Number of years of ownership

Eq. 1   The Grand Unification Theory of Real Estate Profit and Loss:
Net Profit =
$$P \times [(1 + A)^N - (1 + (I_m \times N))] + D \times [(I_m - I_i) \times N]$$

Eq. 2   The Down Payment Coefficient:
$$(I_m - I_i) \times N$$

Eq. 3   The Leverage Factor:
$$P/D$$

Eq. 4   The Purchase Price Coefficient:
$$(1 + A)^N - (1 + (I_m \times N))$$

As detailed in Figure 21, four simplifying assumptions were made in deriving the Grand Unification Theory of Real Estate Profit and Loss. The fourth assumption merits further comment. By restricting the home loan to eight years or less, an interest-only loan approximates a fully amortized loan to within 2%. We may therefore assume the mortgage is an interest-only loan, which tremendously simplifies the equation. (Furthermore, to attempt to predict more than a decade into the future, in an area as volatile as real estate, is naive indeed.)

Given the assumptions of Figure 21, the net profit on a home is the selling price of the home minus the following five items: (1) the total after-tax interest payments on the mortgage; (2) the total after-tax interest lost by tying up the down payment money in a house; (3) the down payment; (4) the loan balance; (5) the total principal payments. But notice that the last three items simply add up to the purchase price of the home. Therefore, the net profit on a home can be defined more simply as the selling price minus the total after-tax mortgage interest, the total after-tax interest lost on the down payment, and the purchase price. By deriving the equations and manipulating terms, we arrive at the expression for net profit shown in equation 1 of Figure 21.

So, by staring at equation 1, do you feel you have conquered the kingdom of real estate? No? Well then let's take equation 1 and see if by tearing it apart we can gain insight into the formidable world of profit and loss.

Let's step back and look at equation 1 in general terms. First, when the equation yields a positive number, then you have earned more money upon selling than you have spent while owning the property--i.e., you made some net profit. Second, notice the two basic components to the equation: The term farthest to the right multiplies the down payment by a bracketed expression and the term to the left multiplies the purchase price by a bracketed expression. Next, note that after-tax interest rates are used in the expression. Tax has an equal impact on both the mortgage interest (I_m) and the investment interest (I_i). The interest you pay on your mortgage is reduced by your tax bracket, and the interest you earn on your investment is similarly reduced. This analysis will always use effective (i.e., after-tax) interest rates. Fourth, you know some people actually *lose* money in real estate. Therefore, you would expect to see some *minus* signs in the equation, and indeed there are. The whole trick to making a profit is to make the positive terms of equation 1 outweigh the negative terms.

Now let's explore equation 1 in more detail. You can see that each of the bracketed expressions in equation 1 may be positive or negative. When one of the bracketed expressions is positive, then its associated variable (either down payment or purchase price) has a positive affect on net profit. And vice-versa. Therefore, by investigating the two terms of equation 1 individually, we can determine the conditions under which profit increases by purchasing a more expensive home and the conditions under which profit increases by increasing the down payment. Since the down payment term is simpler, let's investigate it first.

In equation 1, let's refer to the expression that multiplies the down payment as "the down payment coefficient." This coefficient is shown in equation 2.

By examining the down payment coefficient it is evident that if the interest you are currently making on the money to be used for the down payment (I_i) exceeds the interest on the loan (I_m), then the down payment coefficient is negative and your net profit increases with decreasing down payment. In other words, this term states what is intuitively obvious: If the interest on your current investment exceeds the interest on the home loan, keep your down-payment money in your investment. Therefore, put down less money and borrow more. If the interest on your current investment is less than the interest on the home loan, put down more money and borrow less. Simple!

There, in one fell swoop, we have demystified the entire "no-money-down" movement! Putting down less money does not automatically yield higher profits. In fact, if the interest on the home loan equals the interest you are currently earning on the money to be used for the down payment, then the down-payment coefficient

goes to zero, and your down payment, large or small, has
no impact on your net profit! Put down nothing or pay
full cash--if the interest rate on your investments
approximates the interest rate of the mortgage, your net
profit does not change.

But by putting down less money you are higher
leveraged and, as proclaimed in numerous books and
articles, the higher you are leveraged, the greater your
profit. Am I suggesting that leverage has nothing to do
with profit? Yes! Am I suggesting that these real estate
experts from time immemorial are wrong? Yes!

These experts have forgotten some physics concepts
that you understood quite well as a kid. Remember the
Sunday family outings to the park? One of the many
delightful amusements in the children's play area is the
teeter-totter. But unlike the swings, the teeter-totter
requires two people to play. This presents a problem.
Your creepy brother, who would normally never play
with you, seems extremely willing to play. Suspiciously
willing. Having already exhibited his despicable moral
fabric in the Lincoln Log Incident, you fear he might
jump off the seesaw while you are six feet in the air. So
you ask Mom to play instead. "Oh honey I'm so much
bigger than you it will never work," she responds. You
sigh, and politely explain that the Parks and Recreation
District has anticipated this situation, and has provided a
variable fulcrum point. The two of you adjust the seesaw,
giving Mom the shorter side and you the longer. You
seesaw happily together, until you jump off with Mom
six feet in the air.

The teeter-totter is a classic lever, and you intuitively
understood how to use a little (your weight) to lift a lot
(Mom's weight) through leverage. As shown in
Figure 22, the analogous situation in real estate is to use
a little (your down payment) to buy a lot (your house) by
using the mortgage as a lever arm. Figure 22 easily
translates into a simple leverage formula. We can define
a "leverage factor" as the ratio of the purchase price to
the down payment (see equation 3). Leverage increases
as "P" increases or as "D" decreases.

Figure 22. Leverage

Now returning to the net profit formula (eq. 1), the purchase price "P" does indeed appear in the equation, as does the down payment "D," but they are completely independent variables. In particular, the ratio P/D (the leverage factor) has nothing to do with determining profit or loss!

Leverage is defined by the California Department of Real Estate as "the use of debt financing of an investment to maximize the return per dollar of equity invested." Translated, this says that leverage is "investing less to make more," which we have shown to be misguided thinking. Like other experts in the field of leverage, the California Department of Real Estate has fallen into the "return-on-investment" trap. Their reasoning goes something like this: "This $100,000 home is going to appreciate 10% this year to $110,000. Therefore, if I put down $20,000 I make a 50% return on my investment, but if I put down $10,000 I make a 100% return." This naive analysis obviously fails to consider interest payments on the loan. Once all the ramifications are considered, you soon realize that the down payment impacts your net profit only to the extent that the mortgage interest rate differs from the interest you are earning on your current investments.

To end the confusion and misinformation, I propose a new definition of leverage, one more in keeping with the spirit of the teeter-totter: "Leverage is the ratio of purchase price to down payment." This definition removes any attempt to draw a correlation between leverage and profit.

Already you've worn your number 2 pencil to the stub, and we've just begun! What else can equation 1 tell us? Lots. The other term in the equation multiplies "P," the purchase price, by a terrifying mathematical nightmare. But that nightmare is fundamental to the American Dream, so let's grapple with it.

The expression that multiplies "P" shall be referred to as the "Purchase Price Coefficient," and is shown in equation 4. When it is positive net profit increases with increasing purchase price. When the coefficient is negative you will probably lose money on the deal, and you should question the wisdom of purchasing the property in the first place. (Once rent savings are considered this may change, but we are keeping things simple for now.)

So net profit increases with increasing purchase price if the Purchase Price Coefficient is positive. Equation 4 contains only three variables:

1. the after-tax interest rate on the loan
2. the appreciation
3. the number of years the home is owned

These three simple factors are at the heart of every tycoon's feast or famine in real estate.

Does equation 4 make intuitive sense? Yes! For example, in the simple case where you've owned the home one year ($N = 1$), equation 4 says a larger purchase price will yield a higher profit if:

$$(1 + A)^1 > [1 + (I_m \times 1)] \quad \text{or} \quad A > I_m.$$

In other words, if appreciation exceeds the interest rate, and you hang onto the home at least one year, you make a higher profit by purchasing a more expensive home. This seems to make sense.

But what if appreciation is less than the interest rate? It can be shown that as long as the appreciation is greater than zero, and you hang onto the home long enough, you will *always* make more money purchasing a more expensive property. This is a startling statement, but it is simply the happy consequence of compounding appreciation. So that house that seems like a money drain this year may actually yield a net profit if you hang onto it long enough. However, keep in mind that "long enough" may in some situations be decades! You may not want to wait that long before reaping the profits.

We have a word--leverage--to describe the bogus concept of increasing your profit by increasing your purchase-price-to-down-payment ratio. Unfortunately, there is no word to describe the correct concept of increasing your net profit by increasing the Purchase Price Coefficient. But let's not kowtow to the English language. We'll just invent a word. The Purchase Price Coefficient is so fundamental to the potential profit or loss from a given property that I shall christen it with a name more in keeping with its stature. I hereby knight thee "Real Estate Profitability Expression." But since at this point we're all feeling intimate with the expression, we'll just call it REPE for short.

Are you totally perplexed? Perhaps it would help to summarize The Grand Unification Theory of Real Estate Profit and Loss with some rules of thumb:

1. Profit is not simply the selling price minus the purchase price. A realistic profit picture must include costs while owning the home. Two of the most substantial expenditures while owning a home are the mortgage interest payments and the interest lost by tying up the down payment in a house.

2. Ignoring non-mortgage costs, such as closing costs and property maintenance, and ignoring savings such as rent savings, your profit upon selling a home is determined by:
   a. initial purchase price
   b. appreciation
   c. down payment
   d. number of years of ownership
   e. mortgage interest rate
   f. investment interest rate

3. Within the assumptions outlined in rule 2 above, you lose money on a home if The Grand Unification Theory of Profit and Loss (equation 1) yields a negative number.

4. If the appreciation rate is positive, your net profit becomes increasingly larger (or your net loss increasingly smaller) the longer you own the home. In fact, if the appreciation rate is positive, you will always realize a net profit if you hang on to the home "long enough."

5. If the interest rate on your current investment exceeds the interest rate on the loan, put down less and borrow more. Conversely, if the interest rate on the loan exceeds the interest rate on your current investment, put down more and borrow less.

6. Except for the considerations outlined in rule 5, the ratio of the purchase price to down payment does not influence net profit.

7. If the REPE is positive, you realize higher profits by purchasing a more expensive home.

8. If the appreciation rate exceeds the mortgage interest rate, the REPE is always positive.

9. Due to its exponential affect, appreciation has the most dramatic impact on net profit.

Well, do these equations all seem so neat and tidy that they couldn't possibly be true? What about the hundreds of issues not accounted for by the equations, like closing costs, rent savings, annual property tax, or a new roof? As a tool for comparing different investment opportunities, all the additional expenses can be ignored without too much worry because they won't vary dramatically from house to house.

The physicists struggling with the grand unification of relativity and quantum mechanics actually have an easier task than we do, for they don't need to factor in the Human Element. For example, how does one incorporate into an equation the fact that potential home buyers of your place in Tracy don't seem to appreciate the phallic-shaped swimming pool you added last year? Likewise, even new math can't predict the five buyers frantically bidding against each other for the opportunity to one day cut *their* tomatoes on your blue-tile kitchen counter.

These equations simply provide a method of gaining some perspective on the confusing world of profit and loss. But since mathematics cannot predict earthquakes, school district re-zoning, or the effect of blue tile on a potential home buyer, these formulas should all be taken with a grain of salt. Despite its limitations, The Grand Unification Theory of Real Estate Profit and Loss is far better than the often misleading, anecdotal "theories" offered by real estate experts to date.

For further assistance, reference 155 analyzes a property's investment potential.

APPENDIX II

BAY AREA APPRECIATION

Look at Figure 23. You happen to be looking for your first home in Sonoma County. Does Figure 23 depress you? Or perhaps you have restricted your housing search to San Mateo County. Does Figure 23 excite you? If you answered yes to either question, then this book has failed to impart two basic concepts about home buying. First, appreciation varies dramatically from neighborhood to neighborhood. In Sonoma you can find neighborhoods where appreciation matches and even exceeds the average appreciation of San Mateo. Similarly, some areas of San Mateo County cannot match even the average appreciation of Sonoma County. Second, you will be miserable sitting in your wildly appreciating San Mateo condominium if you had your heart set on the green rolling hills of Sonoma.

Furthermore, statistical analysis is an exact science as long as there is exactly one source of statistics. But get two or more institutions analyzing the same area and they are sure to derive different conclusions. For example, The Office of Thrift Supervision sets appreciation in the Bay Area for 1989 at about 5%, whereas the California Association of Realtors (CAR) gives a Bay Area appreciation rate of over 20% for the same period. Even our innocent looking Figure 23 suffers scars from the War of the Numbers. It indicates a 1983 to 1988 Bay Area appreciation of 10.3%. But none of the individual Bay Area counties score an appreciation rate above 9.5%. How can this be? Easy: The Bay Area statistics are from CAR; the county statistics are from Dataman.

So while Figure 23 is interesting, I hope it has no impact on your housing search. You are fortunate in that it is difficult to actually lose money on Bay Area real estate. Aside from following the basic cautionary guidelines described in this book, you can let your heart be your guide. Thanks to the strong Bay Area housing market, appreciation will take care of the itself.

Figure 23.
Bay Area Appreciation
(over five years from 1983 to 1988)

Area (by county)	Median Selling Price 1983	1988	Annual Appreciation
Alameda	99,000	150,000	8.6%
Contra Costa	94,000	141,000	8.4%
Marin	144,000	218,000	8.6%
San Francisco	N/A	253,000	N/A
San Mateo	127,000	200,000	9.5%
Santa Clara	112,000	168,000	8.4%
Sonoma	86,000	128,000	8.3%
Bay Area	132,000	215,000	10.3%
California	113,000	166,000	8.0%

Sources: California Association of Realtors and Dataman Information Services.

REFERENCES AND RESOURCES

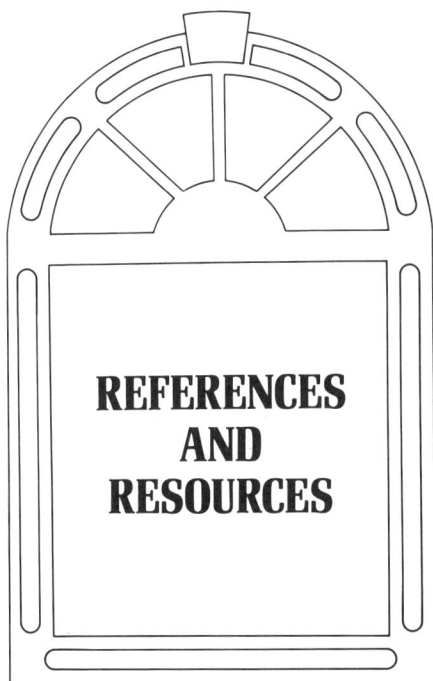

General Real Estate Information

-Books-

1. Bloch, Sonny. *Inside Real Estate*. Weidenfeld and Nicolson, 1987. $18.95.
   Consumer-oriented information on home buying and selling.
2. Bruss, Robert. *Smart Investor's Guide to Real Estate*. Crown Publishers, 1985. $15.95.
   Great source of information on conventional and unconventional financing written by one of the sharpest people in the field.
3. *Realty Blue Book.* Professional Publishing Corporation, 122 Paul Drive, San Rafael, Calif. 94903. (415) 472-1964. $22.00.
   Annual publication includes realty finance tables, purchase offer clauses, explanations of various mortgage instruments, and much more.

-Publications-

4. Agriculture and Natural Resources Publications, 6701 San Pablo Avenue, University of California, Oakland, Calif. 94608-1239. (415) 642-2431.
    Ask for publications catalog. Brochures on everything from shopping for loans to economic trends in the honey industry.

5. Bank of America, local branches.
    There are four "Consumer Information Reports" of interest to home buyers: (a) Steps to Buying a Home; (b) A Guide to Selling Your Home; (c) Planning Home Improvements; (d) Shopping for Adjustable-Rate Credit.

6. California Association of Realtors, 525 South Virgil Avenue, Los Angeles, Calif. 90020. (213) 739-8227.
    Request publications catalog.

7. Center for Real Estate and Urban Economics, 2680 Bancroft Way, Suite A, University of California, Berkeley, Calif. 94720. (415) 642-0224.
    Ask for current publications list.

8. Consumer Information Center, P.O. Box 100, Pueblo, Col. 81002. (719) 948-3334.
    Request their catalog of consumer guides.

9. Department of Housing and Urban Development, Library and Information Services, 451 7th Street S.W., Room 8141, Washington, D.C. 20401. (202) 755-6420.
    Request their free publications by specifying an area of interest, such as home buying, condominiums, financing, rehab or programs of HUD.

10. Office of Thrift Supervision, Information Services, 801 17th Street N.W., Washington, D.C. 20552. (202) 416-2751.
    Publications on everything from co-ops to ARMs. Request publications list.

11. Federal Reserve Bank, Public Information, P.O. Box 7702, San Francisco, Calif. 94120. (415) 974-3230.
    Ask for publications list, "Public Information Materials."
12. Government Printing Office Bookstore, 450 Golden Gate Avenue, San Francisco, Calif. 94102. (415) 556-0642.
    Order "Homes" (subject bibliography #41), which lists government publications pertaining to housing.
13. Inter-City Express, 125 12th Street, Oakland, Calif. 94607. (415) 465-3121.
    Real estate newspaper published every weekday. Each day has a different focus: Monday, foreclosures; Tuesday, real estate profession; Wednesday, investing; Thursday, law and taxes; Friday, lending.
14. Newspaper Books, 64 East Concord Street, Orlando, Florida 32801. (800) 322-3068.
    Ask to be sent publication list of Robert Bruss' excellent reports.

-Seminars and Classes-
15. Bay Area Investors Educational Services, P.O. Box 20866, Oakland, Calif. 94620. (415) 339-9014.
    Ask to be sent their newsletter. Some workshops, of interest to first-time buyers, are open to nonmembers for a fee.
16. Castle Seminars, 3020 Bridgeway Blvd., Suite 166, Sausalito, Calif. 94965. (415) 388-6766.
    Offers seminars throughout the Bay Area for first-time buyers. $20 to $45 plus $8 materials fee. Also provides equity-sharing education and services, as well as a real estate agent referral service.
17. Learning Annex, 2500 Clay Street, San Francisco, Calif. 94115. (415) 922-9900.
    Free guide includes real estate seminar listings.

18.   Open Exchange, P.O. Box 9654, Berkeley, Calif. 94709. (415) 526-7190.
       Free guide includes real estate seminar listings.
19.   Real Estate Information and Networking Group, P.O. Box 70958, Sunnyvale, Calif. 94086. (408) 988-8500.
       Ask to be sent monthly newsletter listing seminars and information from a variety of sources, with a focus on equity sharing and foreclosures.
20.   UC Berkeley Extension, 2223 Fulton Street, Berkeley, Calif. 94720. (415) 642-4111.
       Offers many short courses in both Berkeley and San Francisco on subjects ranging from partnerships to restoration.

Community Colleges and Adult Education

The following community colleges offer a course entitled "Principles of Real Estate," which is appropriate for first-time buyers. In addition, their Community Education Departments occasionally hold seminars for first-time buyers.

Most Bay Area communities also have adult education programs that offer real estate seminars. Finding these adult schools in the phone book isn't easy. For example, in San Francisco they are listed in the government listings under "Schools--Colleges and Adult Education," whereas in Berkeley they are listed in the white pages under "Berkeley Public Schools."

The following list focuses on Bay Area Community College Districts (CCD).

21.   Contra Costa CCD.
       Each campus has its own schedule and its own Community Services Department.
       Contra Costa College, San Pablo. (415) 235-7800.
       Diablo Valley College, Pleasant Hill. (415) 685-1230.
       Los Medanos, Pittsburg. (415) 439-2181.

22. Chabot CCD. (415) 786-6600.
    Call district office for comprehensive schedule.
    Chabot College, Hayward. (415) 786-6600.
    Chabot College, Livermore. (415) 455-5300.
23. Foothill/DeAnza CCD.
    Class schedule covers both campuses. Community
    Services Department has its own schedule.
    Community Services. (415) 960-4373.
    DeAnza College, Cupertino. (408) 996-4760.
    Foothill College, Los Altos Hills. (415) 960-
    4600.
24. Fremont/Newark CCD.
    The Community Services Department schedule is
    listed in the regular schedule of classes.
    Ohlone College, Fremont. (415) 659-6000.
25. Marin CCD.
    Class schedule and catalog is sent to all Marin
    residents. Community Education has a separate
    schedule.
    Community Education. (415) 485-9305.
    College of Marin, Kentfield. (415) 485-9411.
26. Peralta CCD. (415) 466-7200.
    Call their district office for a schedule covering
    all their campuses. Community Education courses
    are listed in the rear of the schedule.
    College of Alameda. (415) 522-7221.
    Merritt College, Oakland. (415) 531-4911.
    Vista College, Berkeley. (415) 841-8431.
27. San Francisco CCD. (415) 239-3070.
    Their centers, located throughout San Francisco,
    occasionally offer seminars in real estate. Call the
    district office for a comprehensive schedule. City
    College has a separate schedule.
    San Francisco City College. (415) 239-3000.
28. San Jose CCD. (408) 274-6700.
    Call district office for schedule covering both
    campuses.
    Evergreen College, San Jose. (408) 274-7900.
    San Jose City College. (408) 298-2181.

29.   San Mateo County CCD.
        Each campus has a separate schedule. The
        Community Education schedule is also separate.
            Community Education. (415) 574-6563.
            Canada College, Redwood City. (415) 364-
            1212.
            San Mateo College. (415) 574-6161.
            Skyline College, San Bruno. (415) 355-7000.
30.   West Valley Joint CCD. (408) 867-2200.
        Call the district office for a comprehensive
        schedule. The Community Development
        Department has a separate schedule.
            Community Development Department. (408)
            867-0440.
            Mission College, Santa Clara. (408) 988-2200.
            West Valley College, Saratoga. (408) 867-
            2200.

Government Programs

-Federal-

31.   Department of Housing and Urban Development
        (HUD), 450 Golden Gate Avenue, San Francisco,
        Calif. 94102. (415) 556-5900.
            Ask for the general information packet on the
            Federal Housing Administration. Included is
            information on FHA loans and closing costs.
            The classified section of the Sunday *Examiner*
            lists repossessed homes that HUD has for sale,
            and the information packet explains how to
            purchase HUD foreclosures.
32.   Veterans Administration, 211 Main Street, San
        Francisco, Calif. 94105. (415) 495-8900.
            Ask for pamphlet 26-4. Also ask for current
            list of VA repossessed homes. For pre-
            recorded messages covering a variety of
            veteran-related issues phone (415) 974-0138.
33.   Office of Historic Preservation, Department of
        Parks and Recreation, P.O. Box 942896,
        Sacramento, Calif. 94296-0001. (916) 445-8006.
            Information on tax credits for rehabilitating
            historic buildings.

34. Farmers Home Administration, 194 Main Street, Suite F, Woodland, Calif. 95695-2915. (916) 666-3382.
    Provides home improvement and home purchase low-interest loans for families who can't qualify for conventional loans. Limited to rural communities of less than 10,000 people. Ask for the Rural Housing Section.

-State-

35. California Housing Finance Agency (CHFA), 1121 L Street, 7th Floor, Sacramento, Calif. 95814. (916) 322-3991.
    Request list of lenders and developers participating in the Home Mortgage Purchase Program. These fixed-rate loans carry interest rates below 9% and require 5% down. The qualifying ratio on these assumable loans is 28%/36%. The Self-Help Housing Program arranges owner-builder projects.
36. Cal-Vet, 2520 Stanwell Drive, Suite 160, Concord, Calif. 94520. (800) 952-5626.
    These programs are different from VA loans. The interest rate varies over the life of the loan. It is currently at 8%. Also, Cal-Vet actually supplies the loan; it doesn't simply guarantee the loan.
37. Rural California Housing Corporation, 2125 19th Street, Suite 101 W., Sacramento, Calif. 95818. (916) 442-4731.
    Works with the Farmers Home Administration assisting low-income home buyers to build their own homes in special rural housing projects.

-Local-

38. Alameda County Planning Department, Housing and Community Development Program, 224 West Winton Avenue, Room 169, Hayward, Calif. 94544. (415) 670-5799.

The Mortgage Credit Certificate Program allows first-time buyers an income tax credit based on interest payments. Lenders may consider this credit when qualifying buyers for a loan.

39. Berkeley Housing Rehabilitation Office, 2180 Milvia Street, Berkeley, Calif. 94704. (415) 644-6590.
    Rental rehab program provides deferred payment loans of up to $8,500.

40. Oakland Office of Community Development, 1417 Clay Street, Oakland, Calif. 94612. (415) 273-3056.
    Request the "OCD Housing Programs" pamphlet listing over 20 housing programs, from rehab loans to shared housing.

41. Contra Costa County Office of Community Development, 651 Pine Street, Martinez, Calif. 94553. (415) 646-2035.
    The Mortgage Revenue Bond Program features interest rates below 9% with 5% down. Rehab loans also available.

42. Contra Costa County, Neighborhood Preservation Program, P.O. Box 749, Martinez, Calif. 94553. (415) 646-2337.
    Housing rehabilitation loans up to $20,000 carry 3% to 10% interest.

43. City of Richmond, Housing and Community Development Department, 330 25th Street, Richmond, Calif. 94804. (415) 620-6720.
    Home improvement loans carry interest rates from 0% to 9%.

44. Richmond Housing Services, 2131 Hoffman Blvd., Richmond, Calif. 94804. (415) 237-6459.
    Private nonprofit organization assists low-income families in obtaining both purchase and rehab loans.

45. Marin County Housing Authority, P.O. Box 4282, San Rafael, Calif. 94913. (415) 472-3602.

Four programs available: For a $15 annual fee, the Below Market Rate Program sends information throughout the year on low-cost condominiums that occasionally become available. Buyers are selected by drawing. Their rehab program offers property improvement loans up to $25,000 with interest from 4% to 10%. The DUO program assists homeowners in adding second living units to their property. Finally, the Mortgage Credit Certificate Program allows first-time buyers an income tax credit based on interest payments. Lenders may consider this credit in qualifying buyers for loans.

46. San Francisco Mayor's Office of Housing, 100 Larkin Street, San Francisco, Calif. 94102. (415) 558-2881.

Request information on first-time home buyer programs. Programs include below-market price condominium projects and low interest, low down payment loans. Rehab loans also available.

47. San Francisco Redevelopment Agency, 939 Ellis, San Francisco, Calif. 94109. (415) 771-8800.

The Affordable Condominium Program keeps monthly housing costs down in exchange for part of the profit upon selling. The Expandable Homes Program assists in the purchase of small, but expandable, homes.

48. San Mateo County Housing and Community Development, 805 Veterans Blvd., Suite 322, Redwood City, Calif. 94063. (415) 363-4412.

Rehabilitation loans from 3% to 6% available in various target areas. Maximum loan is $35,000. The Mortgage Credit Certificate Program allows first-time buyers an income tax credit based on interest payments.

49. Menlo Park Department of Housing and Redevelopment, 701 Laurel Street, Menlo Park, Calif. 94025. (415) 858-3414.

In target areas, rehab loans up to $30,000 are available with interest rates from 3% to 6%.

50. San Mateo City Community Development Department, 330 West 20th Avenue, San Mateo, Calif. 94403-1388. (415) 377-3390.

    Request information on their low- to medium-income first-time buyer developments.

51. Santa Clara County Housing and Community Development Program, 70 West Hedding Street, San Jose, Calif. 95110. (408) 299-2566.

    Request "Community Development Block Grant" brochure, which outlines numerous programs. Rehab loans up to $30,000 carry interest rates from 0% to 9%.

52. Santa Clara County Office of the County Executive, 70 West Hedding Street, San Jose, Calif. 95110. (408) 299-4711.

    Mortgage Credit Certificate Program allows first-time buyers an income tax credit of 20% of interest payments. The lender may considered the credit in qualifying a borrower for a loan.

53. Palo Alto Housing Improvement Program, 250 Hamilton Avenue, Palo Alto, Calif. 94301. (415) 329-2513.

    For low-income households, loans up to $25,000 at 5% interest are available for home rehabilitation. Also, the Energy Services Department offers Residential Conservation Loans up to $1,000 for home insulation.

54. San Jose Department of Neighborhood Preservation, 4 North Second Street, Suite 950, San Jose, Calif. 95113. (408) 277-4747.

    Currently no programs available, but contact them for recent updates.

55. Sunnyvale Housing Division, 456 West Olive Avenue, P.O. Box 3707, Sunnyvale, Calif. 94086. (408) 730-7250.

    Request "Property Improvement Programs" brochure. Fully amortized 15-year loans available for housing rehabilitation. Loan limit of $35,000 on these 4% or 7% fixed-rate loans.

Real Estate Agents

56. California Department of Real Estate, 185 Berry, Room 5816, San Francisco, Calif. 94107. (415) 557-2136.
    Phone them to determine whether disciplinary action has ever been taken against a particular agent or to file a complaint against an agent.
57. Bregman and Miller. *Buyer's Brokerage: A Practical Guide for Real Estate Buyers, Brokers, and Investors.* Tremont Press, 14 Saddlerock Court, Silver Spring, Maryland 20902. (301) 593-0970. 1986. $6.95.
    Short but thorough explanation of "buyer's brokers."
58. *Buyer's Brokers Registry.* Who's Who in Creative Real Estate, P.O. Box 23275, Ventura, Calif. 93002. (805) 643-2337.
    The national directory costs $25, but for $5 you can receive the names of three buyer's brokers in your area. All recommended brokers meet strict qualifying guidelines.
59. *Who Is My Client.* National Association of Realtors, 430 N. Michigan Avenue, Chicago, Ill. 60611. $1.
    Although aimed at realtors, the pamphlet provides an excellent discussion of real estate agent representation.

Cooperative and Shared Housing

-Publications-

60. California Policy Seminar, University of California, Berkeley, Calif. 94720. (415) 642-5514.
    "Limited Equity Housing Co-ops; A Proposal for Legislative Reform" includes a resource guide to co-ops in California. Call for price.
61. Clifford and Warner. *The Partnership Book.* Nolo Press, 1987. $18.95.
    Appropriate for those considering shared ownership.

62. Irwin, Robert. *Mingles.* McGraw-Hill, 1984. $16.95.
     Thorough investigation of shared ownership.

-Organizations-
63. Alternatives Center, 2375 Shattuck Avenue, Berkeley, Calif. 94704. (415) 644-8336. Assists in all phases of developing limited-equity cooperatives.
64. Art House, 1095 Market Street, #820, San Francisco, Calif. 94103. (415) 431-0556. Assists artists and art organizations in finding and developing live-work and studio space.
65. California Cooperative Development Foundation, 1442A Walnut Street, Berkeley, Calif. 94709. (415) 538-0454.
     Educational resource on developing co-ops. Request catalog and seminars listing.
66. City Living, 3295 Clay Street, San Francisco, Calif. 94115. (415) 776-3200.
     Assists in the creation of shared ownership of pre-existing multi-unit buildings.
67. Community Economics, 1904 Franklin Street, Suite 900, Oakland, Calif. 94612. (415) 832-8300.
     Assists community and tenant groups in all phases of arranging low-income group housing. Request publications list.
68. Innovative Housing, 325 Doherty Drive, Larkspur, Calif. 94939. (415) 924-6400.
     Programs include leasing, purchasing, and developing shared-housing communities.
69. McCamant and Durrett, 48 Shattuck Square, Suite 15, Berkeley, Calif. 94704. (415) 848-0331.
     Co-housing workshops, consultations, design services, and referral network.
70. National Association of Housing Cooperatives, 1614 King Street, Alexandria, Va. 22314. (703) 549-5201.
     Request publications list and list of "share-loan" lenders. Primarily a lobbying organi-

zation, but some publications of interest to consumers.

71. National Cooperative Bank Savings Association, 139 S. High Street, Hillsboro, Ohio. 45133. (800) 322-1251.
Provides "share-loan" financing for units in eligible housing cooperatives.

72. Resources for Community Development, 2131 University Avenue, Suite 422, Berkeley, Calif. 94704. (415) 841-4410.
Assists in the creation of limited-equity co-ops and low-income housing in Berkeley.

73. Savings Associations Mortgage Company, 1333 Lawrence Expressway, Suite 330, Santa Clara, Calif. 95051. (408) 985-8110.
Finances "socially oriented" housing projects. The majority of the projects are rentals, but it has financed several limited-equity co-ops.

74. Shared Living Resource Center, 2375 Shattuck Avenue, Berkeley, Calif. 94704. (415) 548-6608.
Workshops and consultations on designing and executing a shared living arrangement.

Shared Equity

-Information-
75. Anderson and Lamb. *Equity Sharing*. Contemporary Books, 1986. $6.95.
Explains the pros and cons of shared equity, and includes sample shared-equity contracts.

76. National Institute of Equity Sharing, 16 West Mission, Suite S, Santa Barbara, Calif. 93101. (805) 687-8097.
Call for names of local real estate agents trained in equity-sharing arrangements.

77. Real Estate Information and Networking Group. See reference 19.

78. Castle Seminars. See reference 16.

79. Newspaper Books. See reference 14.

-Organizations-

The following companies match investors and home buyers. Typically the investor pays a large portion of the down payment in exchange for a large portion of the profits upon selling or refinancing in three to five years. New equity-sharing companies are popping up weekly, so be careful. Talk to at least three companies. From each company get recommendations from three former clients. Have a real estate attorney scrutinize the documents.

80. California Home Equity, Lafayette, Calif. (415) 937-5772.
81. Castle Seminars, see reference 16.
82. Contempo Realty, San Jose, Calif. (408) 448-4488.
83. Eq-U-Share, Cupertino, Calif. (408) 446-5302.
84. Peninsula Estates, Redwood City, Calif. (415) 366-8491.
85. Bruce Roberts Organization, Campbell, Calif. (408) 559-8822.
86. Don Schwartz Real Estate, Capitola, Calif. (408) 476-5454.
87. SECO, San Francisco, Calif. (415) 541-9357.

Credit

88. Bankcard Holders of America, 460 Spring Park Place, Suite 1000, Herndon, Va. 22070. (703) 481-1110.
   Credit information nonprofit organization. Publication subjects include establishing credit for the first time, low-interest-rate credit card list, and repairing bad credit. Request general information packet, which includes the publications list.

When determining a borrower's credit rating, most lenders use credit reports from one of the following credit companies. If, within the past 30 days, you have been refused credit as a result of a company's report, you may receive your credit report from them free. Otherwise, the report costs $8 through the mail.

89.   CBI, P.O. Box 23758, San Jose, Calif. 95153. (408) 224-2900.
90.   Trans Union, P.O. Box 3110, Fullerton, Calif. 92634. (714) 738-3800.
91.   TRW Credit Reports, P.O. Box 8179, Foster City, Calif. 94404. (415) 571-6085.

Mortgages

-Information-
92.   California Mortgage Bankers Association, 1127 Eleventh Street, Suite 534, Sacramento, Calif. 95814. (916) 446-7100.
       Order their free pamphlets, "How to Shop for a Mortgage" and "Consumer Guide to 15 Year Mortgages" by sending a stamped, self-addressed business-size envelope. Their discussion of seller financing is, of course, biased, but the rest is extremely well written.
93.   Fannie Mae Answer Desk, P.O. Box 2614, Pasadena, Calif. 91102-2614. (818) 568-5125 or (818) 568-5463.
       Confused by the rules and regulations of the Federal National Mortgage Association? The Answer Desk staff provides helpful assistance. Also request their free brochures "Consumer Guide to ARMs," "A New ARM for Today's Home Buyer," "Convertible ARMs," and "BiWeekly Mortgage." To receive information on repossessed homes that the Federal National Mortgage Association has for sale, phone or write to them indicating your zip code of interest.

-Mortgage Rate Surveys-
94.   Mortgage Market Weekly, 1125B Arnold Drive, Suite 170, Martinez, Calif. 94553. (415) 372-8808.

Provides mortgage bankers with a computerized data bank of nearly 2000 loan programs. Call for a referral to a "Rates OnLine" subscribing lender.

95.   Title companies, various locations.
Founders Title, First American Title and others publish their own mortgage surveys, available free from local branches.

96.   Local newspapers. See Figure 11.

97.   Real/Net, 1410 Danzig Plaza, Suite 102, Concord, Calif. 94520. (415) 827-3553.
An information service providing mortgage tables to most Bay Area newspapers. For $19.95 you can receive a list of nearly 160 Bay Area lenders and their current rates. Specifies which lenders lock in their rates.

98.   HSH Associates, 1200 Route 23, Butler, New Jersey. 07405. (800) 873-2837.
For $18 they send their Home Buyer's Kit, which includes a guide to choosing mortgages and two weekly "Residential Mortgage Updates," each of which lists the weekly rates of over 60 California lenders. About 20 of the lenders are in the Bay Area. Send SASE for free brochure.

Foreclosures

In addition to the following sources of foreclosed homes, all the government agencies that provide loans also have a stock of foreclosed homes.

99.   Real Estate Information and Networking Group.
An educational resource on foreclosures. See reference 19.

100.   Fannie Mae Properties, see reference 93.

101.   Internal Revenue Service, Seizures and Sales Hotline, Federal Building, San Francisco. (415) 556-5021.
Call for recorded information on foreclosed homes that the IRS has for sale.

102. Resolution Trust Corporation, 550 17th Street N.W., Washington, D.C. 20429. (202) 898-8750. Under the 1989 savings and loan bailout, RTC is responsible for selling off over $100 billion in real estate assets formerly held by the institutions. About 15% of the properties are single-family homes.

Title, Escrow, and Closing

103. California Land Title Association, P.O. Box 13968, Sacramento, Calif. 95853. (916) 444-2647. Many free pamphlets, including "Understanding Closing and Title Costs" and "Understanding Common Ways of Holding Title." Request publications list.
104. Ticor Title Insurance, 50 California Street, 16th Floor, San Francisco, Calif. 94111-4601. (415) 781-3500. Request free brochures "Why You Need Title Insurance" and "What Happens in Escrow."
105. U.S. Department of Housing and Urban Development. See reference 31. Request "Buying a Home? Don't Forget Those Closing Costs."

New Housing

These are the top ten developers in the Bay Area according to a San Francisco *Examiner* survey. Call the builders about current developments and ask to be notified of future developments.

106. Citation Builders, Central/South Bay: (408) 985-6000; North Bay: (415) 372-0300.
107. Kaufman and Broad, Central/South Bay: (800) 662-6926; North Bay: (800) 822-6696.
108. Hofmann, (415) 682-4830.
109. Shea Homes, (408) 279-3770 or (800) 255-6663.
110. Presley, (415) 937-8864.
111. Shapell Industries, (408) 946-1550.
112. Standard Pacific, (415) 847-8700.

113. O'Brien and Hicks, (415) 377-0300.
114. Centex Homes, (415) 228-9890.
115. Dividend Development, (408) 246-5001.

Fixer-Uppers and Construction

116. American Institute of Architects, 130 Sutter Street, San Francisco, Calif. 94104. (415) 362-7397.
     Request their "documents list." Their forms include owner/contractor contracts.
117. Builders Booksource, 1817 Fourth Street, Berkeley, Calif. 94710. (415) 845-6874.
     Unique bookstore specializing in real estate, construction, renovation, landscaping, and architecture.
118. California Manufactured Housing Institute, 10390 Commerce Center Drive, Suite 130, Rancho Cucamonga, Calif. 91730. (714) 987-2599.
     Request their publications list and general information packet for consumers, which includes a list of mobil home and manufactured home retailers. (Also order "How to Buy a Manufactured Home" by sending $.50 to reference 8.)
119. Community Design Center, 1663 Mission Street, Suite 520, San Francisco, Calif. 94103. (415) 863-0730.
     For low-income individuals and nonprofit groups, provides construction advice on additions, improvements, and bringing buildings up to code.
120. Contractors State License Board, 301 Junipero Serra Blvd., Room 206, San Francisco, Calif. 94127. (415) 469-6200.
     Their free pamphlet, "What You Should Know Before You Hire a Contractor," is an excellent guide to choosing a contractor. Also check with them to determine if any legal actions have been taken against a contractor.

121. National Association of the Remodeling Industry, 1901 North Moore Street, Suite 808, Arlington, Va. 22209. (703) 276-7600.
Request "NARI Data Center" publications list.
122. National Association of Home Builders, 15th and M Streets N.W., Washington, D.C. 20005. (202) 822-0200.
Request list of their home-building publications.
123. Owner Builder Center, 1250 Addison Street, Suite 209, Berkeley, Calif. 94702. (415) 848-6860.
Courses offered throughout the Bay Area on house building, renovation, and remodeling. House inspection service also available.
124. Remodeling Magazine, 655 15th Street, N.W., Suite 475, Washington, D.C. 20005. (800) 634-4773.
The annual "Cost vs. Value" report compares the cost of a remodeling project to the added resale value. Make check of $4.50 payable to Hanley-Wood.

Home Inspections and Warranties

125. Hoffman, George. *How to Inspect a House.* Addison Wesley, 1985. $8.95.
Excellent primer on how to scrutinize the physical aspect of a home prior to purchasing.
126. American Home Shield, 90 South E Street, Santa Rosa, 95404. (707) 578-2800.
Provides one-year home warranties covering malfunctions due to normal wear and tear in plumbing, heating, electrical systems and built-in appliances. Call for brochure.
127. American Institute of Real Estate Appraisers, 430 North Michigan Avenue, Chicago, Ill. 60611-4088. (312) 329-8559.
Request four free publications: (a) Estimating Home Value; (b) Analyzing Rehab Potential; (c) Planning Home Improvements; (d) Understanding the Appraisal.

128. American Society of Home Inspectors, 3299 K Street, N.W., 7th Floor, Washington, D.C. 20007. (202) 842-3096.
      Request their free brochures "Enter the Home Inspector" and "Home Inspection and You."

129. Environmental Protection Agency, Office of Air and Radiation, 215 Fremont Street, San Francisco, Calif. 94105. (415) 974-8201.
      Why be happy when you could be worrying about radon? "A Citizen's Guide to Radon" explains what it is and "The National Radon Measurement Proficiency Program" lists government-approved radon testing companies.

130. Home Owners Warranty Corporation, 909 East Las Colinas Blvd., Suite 1300, Irving, Texas. 75039. (800) 433-7657.
      Ask for the pamphlet "Home Buyer's Guide to HOW."

131. Home Buyers Warranty, 1651 East Fourth Street, Suite 219, Santa Ana, Calif. 92701. (800) 821-0429.
      Request their free pamphlet describing their new home warranties.

132. Structural Pest Control Board, 1430 Howe Avenue, Sacramento, Calif. 95825. (916) 920-6323.
      Call to determine if a termite company has a valid license. You may also request a complaint history on as many as three companies. Request their free brochures: (a) Structural Pest Control; (b) Household Pest Control; (c) Fumigation for Pest Control. For $2 they send a copy of any termite inspection report on a specified property done within the last two years.

133. U.S. Consumer Product Safety Commission, 555 Battery Street, Room 401, San Francisco, Calif. 94111-2390. (415) 556-1816.
      Request the asbestos abatement packet.

Bay Area Communities Information

134. Clancy, Lillian. *California Public Schools: How Are They Doing?* California School Surveys, P.O. Box 4901, Walnut Creek, Calif. 94596-9639. (415) 939-8563. $34.95.
   Annually ranks schools and districts based on statewide student tests. Specify "Bay Area Counties."
135. Coldwell Banker, P.O. Box 5125, San Ramon, Calif. 94583. (800) 327-9923.
   "Relocation Guides" give information on home prices, local culture, weather, and much more for various locales nationwide, including the Bay Area.
136. San Francisco *Examiner.*
   Every Wednesday the "Neighborhood Weekly" section lists weekly crime reports, home sales, and much more for San Francisco and the East Bay. Also the "Living In" column in the Sunday real estate section explores different communities every week.
137. McCormack, Don. *McCormack's Guides.* P.O. Box 773, Martinez, Calif. 94553. (415) 229-3581. $5.95 (includes tax and shipping).
   Irreverent annual guides to Alameda, Contra Costa, San Mateo, and Santa Clara counties. Includes school rankings, directory of private schools, crime statistics, and city profiles. Specify county of interest.

Housing Counseling Centers

These agencies are partly funded by HUD. They provide free home-purchase guidance to low- and medium-income buyers. A valuable resource.

138. ECHO Housing Assistance Center, 770 A Street, Room 402, Hayward, Calif. 94541. (415) 581-9380.
139. Housing Service Center, 110 East Gish Road, San Jose, Calif. 95112. (408) 453-3464.

140. Oakland Office of Community Development, 1417 Clay Street, Oakland, Calif. 94612. (415) 273-3056.
141. Pacific Community Services, P.O. Box 1397, Pittsburg, Calif. 94565. (415) 439-1056.
142. Richmond Neighborhood Housing Services, 2131 Hoffman Blvd., Richmond, Calif. 94804. (415) 237-6459.

Low-Income Housing Advocates

143. National Low-Income Housing Coalition, 1012 14th Street, N.W., Suite 1500, Washington, D.C. 20005. (202) 662-1530.
    National advocacy group for low-income housing. No programs or literature for first-time home buyers, yet a group deserving of your membership support.
144. California Right to Housing Campaign, 2000 "O" Street, Suite 230, Sacramento, Calif. 95814. (916) 446-7904.
    A state version of the National Low Income Housing Coalition.

Miscellaneous

145. *Bay Guardian*, 2700 19th Street, San Francisco, Calif. 94110. (415) 824-7660.
    In February or March they publish two "Superlists": "Free Tax Assistance in San Francisco" and "Free Tax Assistance in the East Bay." Superlists may be mail ordered for $1.50 each.
146. Bay Area Residential Investment and Development Group (BRIDGE), 82 Second Street, Suite 200, San Francisco, Calif. 94105. (415) 989-1111.
    Nonprofit organization involved in creating low-income housing for purchase. Call for information on current developments.

147. California Apartment Association, 1414 K Street, Suite 610, Sacramento, Calif. 95814. (916) 447-7881.
Call for information on property owners' associations near you.

148. Community Associations Institute, Oakland Airport Center, 414 Pendleton Way, Oakland, Calif. 94621. (415) 636-1377.
National nonprofit education, research, and lobbying organization serving the needs of condominium associations. Order "The Home Buyer and the Community Association," $1.25 plus tax.

149. Ecumenical Association for Housing, 1510 Fifth Avenue, San Rafael, Calif. (415) 453-4887.
Community organization involved in many low-income housing projects. Ask for current list of projects and programs.

150. Help-U-Sell. 57 West 200 South, Salt Lake City, Utah. 84101. (800) 345-1990.
A reduced-fee national real estate service that assists for-sale-by-owners. Call for their home listing brochure. Offices throughout the Bay Area.

151. Mortgage Bond and Tax Credit Allocation Committee, 915 Capitol Mall, Room 417, Sacramento, Calif. 95814. (916) 324-7419.
Coordinates the Federal Low-Income Housing Tax Credit for California.

152. Tax Credit Information Center, P.O. Box 12859, San Rafael, Calif. 94913. (415) 479-8764.
Assists in cutting through the red tape of obtaining substantial federal tax credits for the acquisition and renovation of low-income rental housing.

153. PMI Mortgage Insurance Company, 601 Montgomery Street, San Francisco, Calif. 94111. (415) 788-7878.
Request their free brochure "Private Mortgage Insurance Q and A."

154.   "Real Estate News," Saturdays, 2-4 p.m., KCBS, 74 AM.
       Phone-in show covers a variety of real estate topics.

155.   Stratosphere Publishing, 7118 Westmoorland Drive, Berkeley, Calif. 94705. (415) 486-1310.
       The author of this book teaches seminars and also provides individual consulting. Call for details. Also, two real estate analysis services are available: Request a "Renting vs. Owning" questionnaire. Complete the form and return it along with $16 for a computerized comparison of renting versus owning. Or, for $38, order *The Window of Affordability: The Software.* The program analyzes potential profit and loss, cash-flow, and renting versus owning. Other capabilities include affordability analysis and amortization tables. For Macintosh, IBM PCs and compatibles. Request a free brochure.

INDEX